Bach
Remedies

and other
flower essences

the transforming
and healing
powers of nature

Bach Remedies

and other flower essences

vivien williamson
with contributions by dr andrew tresidder MB BS MRCGP

photographs by **michelle garrett**

LORENZ BOOKS

Many thanks to Gregory Vlamis, a very special friend, for his continued and unfailing generosity with information, time, love and support throughout this project. Particular thanks to: Julian Barnard and his publishers, Ashgrove of Bath, for permission to quote from The Collected Writings of Edward Bach; Andrew Tessider for putting me forward for the bulk of the project, and for contributing the sections on Emotional Healing, The Bach Combinations and Intuitive Diagnosis; Joanne Rippin, for her support and patience in bringing the book to fruition, and Michelle and Dulcie for the wonderful photographs. Heartfelt gratitude for invaluable support to my parents Marguerite and Peter Lob, and to Jane Stevenson, Rose Titchener, David Walksgrove and Sheila Leeder.

First published in 2000 by Lorenz Books

Lorenz Books is an imprint of Anness Publishing Limited
Hermes House
88–89 Blackfriars Road
London SE1 8HA   www.lorenzbooks.com

© Anness Publishing Limited 2000

Published in the USA by Lorenz Books,
Anness Publishing Inc., 27 West 20th Street,
New York, NY 10011

This edition distributed in Canada by Raincoast Books
9050 Shaughnessy Street
Vancouver
British Columbia V6P 6E5

A CIP catalogue record for this book is available from the British Library

Publisher: **Joanna Lorenz**
Senior Editor: **Joanne Rippin**
Designer: **Lisa Tai**
Photographer: **Michelle Garrett**
Production Controller: **Don Campaniello**
Editorial reader: **Jonathan Marshall**
Typesetter: **Diane Pullen**

10 9 8 7 6 5 4 3 2 1

Note to reader/disclaimer

This book is not intended to replace advice from a qualified medical practitioner. Physical illness – both acute and chronic – nutritional difficulties and environmental stresses can all cause emotional imbalances that may not respond to appropriate flower essence therapy. Flower essences are not medicines and are not intended to work on any physical or medically identifiable condition, neither should they be used to treat psychotic conditions. Please seek a medical opinion if you have any doubts about your health.

Neither the authors nor the publisher can accept any liability for failure to follow this advice.

Picture Acknowledgements
The publishers would like to thank the following picture libraries and photographers for the use of their pictures:
Bruce Coleman Collection: 9br; 19tr; 21tl, bl; 67t; 69tr; 70bl; 92tr. Mary Evans Picture Library: 14tr, bl, br; 15tl; 16bl. The Garden Picture Library: 35t. Gettyone Stone: 8bl; 18bl; 20bl; 21tr, br; 22br; 27tl; 63; 67bl; 69br; 74b; 84tr. Images Colour Library: 8-9t; 66tr. Superstock: 10tr. Vivian Williamson: 5; 15tr, b; 17bl, br; 19m, bl; 20tr; 22tr, m, bl; 23; 24tr; 25tl, mr; 26tr, br; 27bl; 32bl, br; 33t, bl, br; 34tl, tr, b; 35bl, br; 36t, bl; 37tl; 38t, bl, br; 39t, br; 40t, bl, br; 41tl, tr, b; 42t; 43tl, br; 44bl, r; 45tl, tr; 50tm, ml; 52tl; 53tm, tr, b; 54bl, br; 55tm, tr, bl; 56t, ml, mr, b; 57t, ml, mr, b; 58t, ml, mr, b; 59tl, tm, tr, bm, br; 60t, bl, br; 61t; 70; 71tl, tm, tr, ml, mr; 74t; 84bl, mr, br; 89br.

Contents

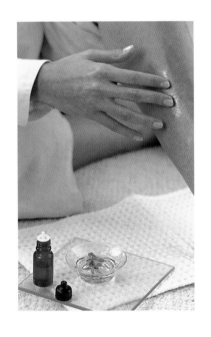

introduction

Many people today live separated from nature, not only in a physical way, but in the mind and heart as well. Flower essences are unique in that they bring the individual back to nature, and supply what is most needed; nurturing systems with the pure, untainted life-force of nature. Flower essences bring about a renewal of positive energy, relaxation and wellbeing.

It was an English physician, Dr Edward Bach (1886–1936) who discovered the healing energies of selected flowering plants and trees. Bach was inspired to turn to nature for gentle, non-invasive and non-toxic essences that would bring harmony and restore balance in the mind and body.

Since 1936, the range of flower essences that Bach developed have been used worldwide by consumers and practitioners, who have reported excellent results. The essences can be used either alone as a healing system, or in conjunction with other methods of healing. Now that they are available in most health-food outlets and pharmacies, anyone can easily benefit from the gentle healing approach of flower essences.

This book aims to provide the reader with a basic, easy-to-use introduction to the Bach flower essences. It also covers a selection of other, more recent essences that work together in harmony with the Bach essences to enhance their qualities, or as single essences. There are detailed explanations of their uses and the suggested indications of the individual essences. The benefits and methods of making flower essences are explained in detail, so that you can share in this powerful, unique and meditative experience of communing with the wholeness of nature. This is intended to be a useful and accessible guide to a simple and gentle method of healing, which, along with the flower essences themselves, can be used to handle life's challenges more effectively.

The term "essence" and "remedy" are interchangeable in the context of Bach flower essences, but for consistency, the former is used throughout the book.

▷ Gentle and versatile, flower essences can be used in any number of creative ways, both internally and externally, to handle life's many and varied challenges.

△ Flower essences are liquid herbal preparations that are simple to use and have no contra-indications. Diluting in water is a quick and accessible way of receiving their benefits.

Emotional healing – healthy mind, healthy body

◁ **The roots of a beech tree look strong, but are actually weak and shallow, like the Beech type.**

Health is harmony of mind, body and spirit – including, of course, healthy emotions – and is also what you achieve when you undergo healing. Healing resolves issues, and puts you into a healthy state of body and mind, a state of being "at ease". Contrast this with being unhealthy, or "dis-eased".

Emotional health is something everyone aspires to, but many cannot attain it without help. Everyone is capable of creating a life which is the true expression of the heart's deepest longing. But in order to stay true to the perfect pattern, you need to listen carefully to your inner feelings.

Sometimes the flow of these feelings becomes blocked within. Your emotions then go out of balance, and your state of emotional health suffers. Emotional health does not mean the absence of strong emotions, such as anger or irritation. The problem arises when these important emotions are held in and repressed, or are expressed but inappropriately. Emotional health comes with the appropriate expression of emotions and their transformation into positive aspects.

We all carry frozen patterns of emotional imbalance within us that cast shadows on our ability to show our true nature. Some of these patterns have a recent origin, some have their roots in the past, in childhood, or even in the womb. Few of us have any insight into our own emotional problems and blockages. In fact, insight into the problem is often the first stage of healing.

emotional transformation

Flower essences are powerful catalysts of emotional transformation. Just as different pieces of music can evoke different emotions, the vibration preserved in a flower essence works as an emotional nutrient to restore emotional balance. Essences work by catalysing a release of outworn and unhelpful emotional patterns and states of mind. Powerfully and gently, they allow frozen patterns of emotion to dissolve, to allow full and complete expression of positive emotional aspects. For example, the Willow essence catalyses the transformation of resentment towards a hard knock into an optimistic approach, and the Holly essence triggers the transformation of jealousy, envy, revenge, suspicion and greed into unconditional love. You might

△ **In the presence of the healing vibrations of a flower essence, affliction** *"melts as snow in the sunshine"*. **Dr Bach,1931**

▷ **Willows can be harshly pollarded, but they continue to grow vigorously. This reflects the renewable and life affirming qualities of this essence.**

be unlikely to choose these for yourself on the basis of such negative emotional qualities, though it may be quite easy to pick out friends or relations who might benefit! However, it is these two essences that you are most likely to be helped by at the start of your journey of emotional healing. The third essence that is often valuable early on is Wild Oat. This essence realigns you to your inner self and helps you find the right path.

▷

the ladder of emotional healing

Why is it so difficult to identify your own emotional needs? The difficulties start in childhood and are carried on through adult life. Small babies have no problems with emotions. They rapidly process emotions to a state of resolution or health – no infant carries layers of accumulated unresolved emotions: if they are wet, cold or hungry, they cry. The cry brings attention, the attention removes the cause of the distress, and all is calm again – until the next emotional challenge.

During childhood, you may have been conditioned into believing that it is not OK to express your emotions. So you adopt habits of burying, repressing or hiding emotional imbalances. This happens almost unconsciously, but has the advantage of allowing you to continue to live life, at least on the surface, without major upset. Unfortunately, buried and unresolved emotions are often even more toxic to long-term health than allowing them to be resolved at the time.

Ask a hundred adults how they feel, and most will say, "Fine. Fine! ..." When you consider the emotional complexities of most lives, you realize that the conventional answer is little more than a thin disguise that helps them to cope with everyday life by means of a little trick called "denial".

Adults rarely express their emotions: what happens instead is a kind of constipation of emotions, a series of emotional

blockages that pile up, layer on layer, like the skins of an onion. From childhood, the gift of spontaneous expression of emotions is steadily shut down by the pressure to conform. The "Nos", "Shouldn'ts" and "Can'ts" of life weigh heavily on us.

Most adults have suffered the lack or withholding of love, as a result of divorce, bereavement, the break-up of a relationship or just the general traumas that occur in the playground called life. Perhaps it is hard to acknowledge the emotional broken glass that we carry, because we accept it as a normal and acceptable part of living.

Emotional imbalances contribute to mental and emotional pain as well as physical ill-health. Studies have shown that expressing emotions and achieving an

△ **Babies express their emotions fully. Adults are conditioned to repress theirs.**

emotional balance helps you live longer and more healthily. Emotional imbalance will influence the tiny molecules of emotion that ebb and flow through the body at the cellular level, in the brain and throughout the body, especially in the gut.

The combination of our mind, body and spirit is finely tuned to always try to restore balance and health. This is just as true for the emotions as for the rest of the body. When the molecules of emotion flow as they should, without blockages, then the "Ladder of Healing" is working. Sometimes, however, you may get stuck on a particular rung – perhaps because of fear, or sadness.

△ **Just as onions have many layers of skins, layers of emotions can build up if not resolved.**

▷ **Given a handful of broken glass, you know what to do. Given a heartful, or a bellyful ...**

THE LADDER OF HEALING, OR RESOLUTION, LOOKS LIKE THIS:

Accept

Acknowledge

Forgive

Release

Move On

To understand the process, and its natural progression, see if you can apply it to an emotional time you have had in the past. See if the stages of the ladder of healing fit the way you progressed through the feelings you experienced at the time.

1 You do not believe it has happened – you are in denial. You have to climb on to the first rung – **Acceptance**.

2 You have to admit to yourself not only that the event has happened, but that it has profound effects on your life that you need to take note of, and integrate into your life. This is the second rung – **Acknowledgement**.

3 The big step comes next – **Forgiveness**. You have to release your anger and frustration at the event, to forgive another person, perhaps – or to forgive yourself for feeling that way. It is this step that is so difficult, and where it is so easy to get stuck. Instead you may project blame outwards ("It was someone else's fault.") or inwards ("If only I'd ..."). The latter becomes guilt.

4 Once you have come this far, **Release**, the next rung, is a relatively easy one and will seem to come quite naturally after Forgiveness.

5 The final step, **Move On**, allows you to integrate the now fully resolved emotional experience into your life.

Emotional healing is a necessity for health, and flower essences are powerful catalysts, allowing healing to occur smoothly, without fuss, and in private.

Bach flower essences

Bach's system was the first system of flower essences to be discovered, and they cover the important basic emotions that everyone is subject to. Bach flower essences are now made by a number of producers all over the world, in accordance with Dr Bach's wishes that his essences should be widely available everywhere. Starting with the Bailey range in Britain and the Flower Essence society range in the USA, there are now well over forty major brands worldwide.

Many people are also discovering the joys of making their own essences. New essences

△ **The flower essences are made from beautiful plants and trees that can do you no harm.**

continue to be discovered as we uncover deeper aspects of ourselves that deserve healing. Perhaps there are as many different aspects to heal as there are essences – and perhaps there are as many essences waiting to be discovered as there are flowers. Flowers have been described as Cosmic Energy Emission Devices, or "CEEDs" and perhaps this profound, cosmic energy can be made available to heal deeper and deeper traumas, personal, ancestral and archetypal.

About Flower Essences

"Flowers have a mysterious and subtle influence upon the feelings, not unlike some strains of music. They relax the tenseness of the mind."

Henry Ward Beecher 1813–87

Flowers in history

Flowers have always been an integral part of life, and are used to celebrate special occasions such as marriages or anniversaries in every culture. They are given with love on Valentine's or Mother's day and as tributes at funerals. Flowers mark the signposts of life and it is easy to respond to their beauty and perfume at a very deep level. Even the smallest and most modest wild flower possesses an amazing power to "move" us.

flower symbolism

In the 19th century, precise meanings were attached to every flower, and lovers would communicate intimate secrets with bouquets; peach blossoms, for example, were a romantic way of saying, "I am your captive." In a strait-laced society, where young women were always strictly chaperoned, flowers were a way of exchanging feelings. "Say it with flowers" is more than just a clever advertising jingle.

△ **Medieval households were self-reliant, collecting and drying their own herbs to prepare remedies.**

flower power

In the 1960s a new culture swept through the youth of the West. The flower children, as they called themselves, gave flowers to everyone, including heads of state, as a message of love and the desire for a more peaceful, co-operative world. Their preoccupation with self-sufficiency stemmed from an urge to return to a life closer to nature.

flowers – therapeutic agents

The Bach flower essences were formulated in the 1930s, but in fact, flower essence therapy has evolved from thousands of years of human interaction with the plant kingdom.

In the past, natural healing agents were discovered through experimentation and by people's intuitive perception of the powers of plants. Further discoveries were made by observing how animals reacted to plants.

People depended on nature for medicinal help, seeking advice from local healers, whose knowledge was passed on through generations. A selection of herbs would be boiled, allowed to cool and drunk over several days. This process, known as decoction, is similar to the boiling method of making a flower essence.

Paracelsus, a 16th-century Swiss physician, was famous for his successful cures. He used the dew from plants to treat emotional problems, believing that all disease originated

with a departure from essential spirituality. Paracelsus felt that the right essence would renew the connection to the spirit within, which is the true healer. This use of dew is closely related to Dr Bach's sun potentization method of making flower essences. There is a saying that dabbling in the dew on May Day will make a woman look more beautiful. This may be more than a myth, as flower essences can develop an inner beauty that brings forth outer beauty.

△ **Paracelsus believed that balancing the four elements created a substance called a quintessence, which healed the soul.**

△ *"Anything green that grew out of the mould was an excellent herb to our fathers of old."* **Kipling.**

△ **Dr Edward Bach turned to nature for remedies that would treat the person rather than the illness or its symptoms.**

△ **The pale mauve flowers of the Impatiens were found to calm impatient, tense and frustrated people.**

flower healing in the 20th century – Dr Edward Bach

Edward Bach (1886–1936) was born in Moseley, Birmingham, of Welsh extraction. His student friends called him "Batch", because they found it awkward to pronounce his name. He became a deep lover of nature from an early age and this played a key role in his life's accomplishments. Bach is reported to have had a keen desire to help others and initially considered going into the clergy before finally choosing to study medicine.

During the early part of his medical career, Bach noticed that while efforts were made to make people more physically comfortable not enough was done to help their feelings; the patient's fear, uncertainty and shock were not addressed in depth. He felt most strongly that these emotions influenced the body and the ultimate well-being of the individual. Beginning his research into finding a simple and certain cure for disease, Bach became a bacteriologist at University College Hospital, London. While there, he collapsed and underwent emergency surgery, and was given just three months to live. However, when partially recovered, he rose from his bed and returned to work, not wishing to waste a moment. Amazingly, Bach slowly gained strength and baffled his physicians with his unexpected recovery. This experience was eventually to form the cornerstone of his system of healing: that health and happiness come from following one's true calling in life.

the influence of homeopathic research

In 1919, Bach joined the staff of the London Homoeopathic Hospital and was delighted to find the ideas of Samuel Hahnemann, the founder of homeopathy, very much in line with his own. Bach developed a range of homeopathically prepared intestinal vaccines, which proved very effective for many

△ **The golden flowered Mimulus was found to give courage to the faint-hearted.**

△ **The creamy white blooms of the Clematis was seen to "wake up" dreamy and sleepy types.**

chronic conditions. Ultimately, they became known as the Seven Bach Nosodes, and are still in use today. Being a keen observer of human nature, he hypothesized that a similar type of person benefited from each of the different nosodes. This led him to the conclusion that the human race was divided into quite clearly defined personality types, so that it was possible to treat an individual according to their particular mental state, rather than their physical condition alone.

Bach was keen to replace the nosodes with herbs, as he preferred not to use the products of disease. In 1928 Bach experimented with three flowers, Impatiens, Clematis and Mimulus. He was overjoyed with the results and decided to give up his practice to concentrate on finding more herbs and to refine his understanding of different mental states.

A new system of healing evolves

From 1930 until his death in 1936, Bach travelled the British countryside. Seeking a new way of preparing his herbs, he observed that ingesting dew had a powerful and positive balancing effect on the system and concluded that the heat of the sun was drawing the healing force of the flower into the droplets of water. Excited at this discovery, but knowing that for many patients collecting dew was not practical or efficient, he duplicated this natural process with his sun potentizing procedure.

Bach's body and mind were becoming very sensitive, and he found that he was able to tune into the vibrations of a particular flower and feel its therapeutic effects. At times, he felt the mental state first and then went into the countryside to find the cure. Eventually, he was able to find an appropriate essence for each of the twelve personality types he had observed, and further essences for other related emotional problems.

completion of the new system

When he was not travelling, Dr Bach spent his time in Cromer on the Norfolk Coast, where he observed the fishermen and holiday-makers to refine his understanding of mental and emotional conditions. Finally, in 1934, with the assistance of a friend, Mary Tabor, he settled in Sotwell, Oxfordshire, where the Bach Centre is still located.

◁ Dr Bach said, all stations in life must be filled, from shop assistant to prince, doctor or artist, and that following the right path will bring fulfilment and happiness.

During his last years, Bach completed the set of 38 essences and started to give lectures on his system of healing. When he died in 1936 he left his "Healing Herbs", as he called them, in the hands of his trusted co-workers, Nora Weeks, Victor Bullen and Mary Tabor who carried on his work until the late 1970s.

◁ Dr Bach liked to study people who lived differently from himself, particularly the fishermen near his home in Norfolk, who were cheerful and happy in their daily lives. This confirmed his growing understanding of personality types.

the philosophy behind Dr Bach's flower healing system

As his research developed, Dr Bach concluded that individuals become ill and unhappy when they stray off their true path in life. He concluded that everyone is born with a unique blueprint for life, whether it is expressed at home, work or play. He believed strongly that all stations or vocations in life were as important as each other, and that whether you were a shop assistant, musician, prince, doctor or artist, it was in following the right path that a person would find true fulfilment, health and happiness. Some fortunate people know what is right for them from an early age, Bach believed, and they are able to follow their hearts faithfully throughout life. However, most get drawn away from their true destiny, as a result of conditioning and the demands of family and society, or by the good intentions of others who may impose their own ideas of what is "best" for them.

> As the Herbs heal our fears, our anxieties,
>
> our worries, our faults, and our failings,
>
> it is these we must seek, and then the
>
> disease, no matter what it is, will leave us.
>
> Edward Bach
> *The Twelve Healers and Other Remedies* (1933)

the primary defects of humanity

In response to such outside interference, and depending on the particular disposition of the individual, negativity may creep into the mind, which can then lead to the manifestations of pride, cruelty, self-love, ignorance, instability, greed or hate. These are the real underlying causes of disease and unhappiness and Bach called them the primary defects. He felt they should be viewed as a message that an individual has strayed away from their blueprint in some way and therefore has something to learn. The true underlying purpose of life is to grow towards perfection, by learning the lessons of life, concentrating on one or two at a time. Dr Bach suggests finding the fault and eliminating it, not by suppression, but by developing the opposing virtue.

▷ **The voice of your intuition may prompt you to consider big changes, or to ask for something as simple as a cup of tea.**

happiness is the key

As these faults are cleansed, a renewed connection to the inner self, or soul, begins to form and, by listening to its awakening voice, it becomes possible to find the true path again. This voice speaks in the way you find it easiest to hear. The voice guides you via desires, intuitions, ideals, likes and dislikes and can lead you through all of life's challenges as long as it is listened to.

Dr Bach emphasized the importance of following a path of love, listening to your inherent goodness, doing no harm to others and allowing everyone perfect freedom to follow their path, as they must allow you the perfect freedom to follow yours. If you feel disapproval from others you should trust your intuition to make your own way. The greatest challenge lies in winning freedom from your closest family members, but, at no point should they be seen as enemies,

rather as worthy companions in the game of life, who are offering you the opportunity to become strong. Do not be afraid, plunge into experiences, embrace a wholly individual approach to life, and remember there is no right or wrong, it is all relative to circumstances. Bach found happiness to be the key, and the gauge by which to measure how closely your life resonates with your soul's blueprint.

△ **Cerato flower essence helps you to hear your inner voice more clearly and trust its message.**

▷ **The Passion Flower essence helps us get in touch with our inner selves, making it easier to listen to the voice of our soul.**

The healing actions of flower essences

Dr Bach described the mechanism of flower essences in a poetic way, saying that, like beautiful music, they lift the spirit. Listening to lovely music can uplift and inspire, and flower essences are consistently reported to produce a similar effect. They are often classified under the umbrella of "vibrational medicine", which makes it easier to understand how the effect of flower essences can be compared to music.

There are many differing opinions on how flower essences work, since it is a subjective, unseen process and many suggest it is not possible to understand completely.

> They [flower essences] are able, like beautiful music, or any gloriously uplifting thing which gives us inspiration, to raise our very natures, and bring us nearer to our Souls: and by that very act, to bring us peace, and relieve our sufferings.
>
> Edward Bach *Ye Suffer From Yourselves* (1931)

balancing the mind-body continuum

Flower essences recharge the system with the life-force of nature. This renewal of energy has a profound healing effect. Each essence is selected as a response to a different negative state of mind and to suit the individual's specific need and character. Perhaps the difficulty in your personality that needs treatment is fear: since the flower essence Mimulus is an embodiment of the energetic blueprint of courage, ingesting it will supply the courage that your personality is lacking.

In addition, through the process of resonance, the influence of Mimulus will form a "bridge" to your higher self, this is where all true potential lies. Mimulus will then re-activate previously inaccessible reserves of courage. In much the same way, a violinist plucking a single string of her instrument can cause all similar strings in the whole orchestra to vibrate with sound.

flower essences as support

The beauty of using flower essences is that they do not interfere with the mind, as chemical drugs do, leaving the person free to grow and solve problems in a healthier way. For example, since the positive virtue of Mimulus is courage, it allows you to turn and face your fears utilizing its energy as support. In time, it becomes possible to dispense with flower essences, as all personal strengths will have been fully retrieved. Depending on the need, a flower essence can give support during times of exhaustion or stress, or strength to face an outside challenge such as an interview or operation. It can be more difficult to confront yourself, but essences will make this easier and give comfort. Should your particular challenge be anger, the Holly essence will be indicated and it will encourage an acceptance and understanding of these strong feelings. If the struggle is with depression, the Gentian essence can bring a lightness of being, making it possible to see things from a new and broader perspective.

◁ *"When solving problems, dig at the root instead of just hacking at the leaves."*
Anthony J D'Angelo. The College Blue Book.

flower essences as transformational catalysts

A catalyst is a substance that enables change to come about, but remains unchanged itself. This is the modern definition of flower essences, as they have been observed to initiate change, guiding the individual from a negative stressful state into a healthier, more affirmative frame of mind. You should never despair of negativity, however, for "within all things are the seeds of their opposite" and a sympathetic resonance, such as the vibration of a flower essence, can restore the true positive state and rebalance the unity of the mind, body and spirit.

flower essences for self-improvement

In the search for wholeness, flower essence therapy is an ideal choice for self-improvement programmes, as it is self-regulating, gently releasing the layers of past conditioning from the outside inwards. Any necessary lessons can be learned and integrated before going on to deeper issues. Flower essences

△ **Three to four hours of clear and cloudless sky is required for the sun to potentize a flower essence.**

can assist the process of self-realization in a gentle way that is comfortable, making it possible to understand and accept the lesson and the need to change. Flower essences, correctly chosen, can continue to give support in the transformation until all personal strengths are fully accessed.

preventive use of flower essences

Flower essences can heal your inner levels, making it possible to become a happier and more joyful individual, which can indirectly improve physical health. Why wait until illness strikes? Let the essences bring your system "up to date" emotionally. The prophylactic benefits of flower essence therapy are often overlooked but are reported by many to be of enormous value.

flower essences, nature's priceless gifts

Flower essences are simple and anyone can appreciate their benefits. They bring about the resolution of everyday stress, inspiring calm, balance, strength, the ability to cope better, solve problems and pace yourself. Flower essences encourage a playfulness of spirit that helps to recharge your batteries and to restore much needed resilience, acting as a buffer against the ups and downs of life. Flower essences can also bring the priceless gift of self-awareness and with it knowledge of your path in life, which is essential to happiness and health. "Feel it to heal it" is a well-known saying, and flower essences can guide you to the realization of your full potential as a human being.

△ **The Gentian flower is a spiritual purple and encourages a renewal of faith.**

▷ **Holly is known as the tree of Christ and the essence encourages love and forgiveness.**

Nature's role in the preparation of flower essences

For much of the history of humanity, alchemists and herbalists have been seeking for healing elixirs. In preparing flower essences, you take on a similar role, being involved in "floral alchemy", reading from the book of Nature and drawing out its essence from its material body. Flower essences are prepared using either of two classical methods: sun potentizing or boiling. They are created using the most beautiful aspect of nature, its flowers. These produce the seeds, which contain the essential energy of the plant, including its complete blueprint for growth.

For the process of sun potentization, the flowers are picked from the plants in a clean, unspoiled environment and fused into a

healing potency. Starting early in the morning, a thin glass bowl is filled with pure water, freshly drawn from a nearby, unpolluted spring and the flowers are floated on the surface. The bowl is left, near where the flowers were growing, in clear sunshine for up to four hours or until the petals have faded. During that time, a metamorphosis will have taken place and the life-force of the flowers will have been "given up" to the water, which may have changed colour, acquired flavour and feel "zingy", if held. This tincture, when preserved in brandy now forms the "mother essence" which will later be diluted to produce the essence.

Some flowering trees that bloom in early spring before the sun is hot are prepared by

△ **Pick early in the day when the flowers are fresh. Choose newly opened blooms, which hold the perfection of living energy.**

boiling the flowers. The resultant liquid is filtered and then also preserved in brandy. The tinctures are diluted to create the flower essence "stocks", which can then be further diluted for individual usage.

the memory of water

How does sun potentization work? Does it have any scientific basis? Recent research by the French scientist Jacques Beneviste, although not universally accepted, has suggested that water can retain the memory of a substance dissolved in it, even when virtually none of the original substance is present. It also remains biologically active: that is, it can produce an effect on the body.

In Beneviste's experiments the water was agitated to produce the effect, and homeopaths believe this research may help to explain how their preparations work. Agitation is not used in the preparation of flower essences. Instead Dr Bach suggests it is the action of the sun that is the catalyst by which the water molecules are fused with the imprint of the flowers used.

◁ **As a bubbling stream filters through the earth and flows down the rocky hillside, the water becomes purified and revitalized.**

the four elements

"It was the method of simplicity he had longed for – the simplicity of mighty things, for fire, earth, air and water – the four elements – were involved and working together to produce healing remedies of great power …

the earth *to nurture the plants*

the air *from which it feeds*

the sun *or fire to enable it to impart its power*

and water *to collect and be enriched with its beneficent healing…"*

Nora Weeks,
The Medical Discoveries of Edward Bach Physician (1983)

The doctrine of signatures

The process of unveiling the healing qualities of a flower essence begins with the doctrine of signatures, which is rooted in medieval cosmology. Physicians of the day used this approach to find healing plants for their patients. The understanding behind this principle is that there is a visible message on the plant, which determines its role in terms of healing. Just as a graphologist can read a person through their writing, so a plant may be read through its growth pattern. This may include the colour of the flowers, root structure, shape of leaves, preferred place of growth, the general shape of the plant, how it fruits, its yearly cycle, historical uses, folklore and so on. The message may be very obvious, as in the case of the Dandelion, which, because the colour is yellow like a jaundiced person, is thought by herbalists to be good for liver problems. It does, in fact, cleanse the body, thereby proving beneficial in such cases.

Modern flower essence makers explore the visual message of the plant, but may also attempt to tune into nature's intelligence to verify the information. This is a very subjective approach and is dependent on how each person views the world. However, the results can be amazingly consistent and are often proven through individual usage.

SOME EXAMPLES OF THE DOCTRINE OF SIGNATURES

• Lungwort leaves with their patches look like lungs, suggesting a use for lung problems.
• Willows, which live in damp places, are indicated for rheumatism, as that condition is aggravated by damp.
• When Comfrey roots are boiled they stick together, so they are often used to knit bones together. Comfrey is also called Knitbone.
• The centre of a Chamomile flower is like a stomach and the plant is thus considered useful for stomach ailments.

△ Comfrey
◁ Chamomile

△ Willow

△ Dandelions have very moist stems if broken, and are sometimes called "piss en lit".

visualization to illustrate the principle of the doctrine of signatures

In your mind, take yourself on a walk through a Bluebell wood: see the dense mass of blue, smell the perfume, feel the cool shade, hear the gentle silence of the wood, taste the freshness of the air. Open up all the senses, let each of them enjoy the experience and just sit for a while. Let your mind reach out to the flowers. Notice how you feel. Look at the Bluebell flowers closely. Does their colour mean calmness to you or does the blue give a feeling of melancholia? The flower heads are hanging down, just as people's heads do when they feel blue. The flowers are very close together – does that suggest protection or an element of stress to you? Spend a few moments assimilating the atmosphere of the wood.

As you return from the wood, what messages do you bring with you? How are you feeling? Uplifted, calm or happy? Clear, and in touch with the best of yourself? Has all stress dissolved? Are you feeling renewed and recharged?

From this example it is possible to see both sides of the picture and get an idea of how to use the Bluebell essence. Given to a stressed and over-wrought person with emotional difficulties, Bluebell brings forth happiness, peace and tranquility. It can also reconnect an individual with their lost sense of self.

exploring the doctrine of signatures

Keeping the doctrine of signatures in mind, notice if a plant catches your attention. Is it possible to observe its message? Maybe the

△ **Bluebell is known as nature's rescue essence, and is supportive for all who are extremely distressed. It is helpful for those suffering from insomnia, depression and tension.**

plant is presenting a totally positive message or a totally negative one, or both, as in the case of the Bluebell. Release your imagination and let it flow, and then out of interest look up other essence makers' descriptions of the same plant and see if their message is similar. If not, is it possible to understand their message? Remember, no one is wrong, everyone has a unique slant on the world and any essence made is co-created with nature and is primarily a healing gift to the self. Exploring the doctrine of signatures is a wonderful and creative way of getting closer to nature and understanding more about flower essences.

The doctrine of signatures for the Bach essences

The doctrine of signatures for the Bach essences has proved to be a complex study, which gives a deep insight into their use and opens the mind in wonder at the intelligence of nature.

Aesculus x carnea, Red Chestnut

The Red Chestnut type worries about others. The red flowering spikes of this tree burst outward, reflecting this emergency state. In this way the Red Chestnut type sends those frightened thoughts out to others.

Aesculus hippocastanum, Chestnut Bud

The sticky sap on the buds of the horse chestnut tree reflects the Chestnut Bud type's tendency to get stuck in repetitive behaviour and thoughts.

Aesculus hippocastanum, White Chestnut

White Chestnut is about worry and the white plumes burst all over the tree, as if the worrying thoughts completely consume the mind of the White Chestnut type.

Agrimonia eupatoria, Agrimony

Agrimony is known as "church steeples", as the flower spikes resemble spires. It grows straight upwards, towards higher realms and the peace that this essence offers to the Agrimony type.

△ Red Chestnut

Bromus ramosus, Wild Oat

Growing beside paths or lanes, the Wild Oat is a tall grass, its head of seeds "hanging around". Similarly, Wild Oat types step off their true path in life and hang around wondering what to do.

Calluna vulgaris, Heather

The Heather plant poisons the soil and can also cover a vast range, discouraging other plants from coming near it. The Heather type can also seem like "poison" and drive away its friends. But heather grows on wide hillsides which encourage a broad view on life, and as the gypsy sells Heather as "lucky", so must Heather types concentrate on the luck in their lives, not the woes.

Carpinus betulus, Hornbeam

One of the most obvious characteristics of the Hornbeam tree is the cooling shade it casts, this makes it ideal for clearing the heavy, fuzzy head of the tired Hornbeam type.

Castanea sativa, Sweet Chestnut

The Sweet Chestnut can live for over a thousand years, observing the births and deaths of many generations. This essence provides the comfort and wisdom of years to those who feel as if they are at the end of the road.

Centaurium umbellatum, Centaury

Just as the Centaury plant is frequently overlooked, so are the needs of the Centaury type. However, it can grow strong and straight where other plants cannot, so ultimately, with the help of this essence, Centaury types will stand up for themselves.

Ceratostigma willmottianum, Cerato

This cultivated plant originates in Tibet, the land of wisdom. Its message for the Cerato type is, trust your inner wisdom and choices, even if they do not fit in with what others think is right.

△ Agrimony

△ Hornbeam

△ **Chicory**

> Little flower, but if I could understand
>
> What you are, root and all, and all in all,
>
> I should know what God and man is.
>
> Tennyson *Flower in the Crannied Wall* (1869)

Chicorium intybus, **Chicory**

Chicory grows beside roads and paths, where life is busiest, so the Chicory type needs to be in on everything that is going on. Its root reaches deep into the earth for nourishment, so this essence helps Chicory types look deeper within for what they need.

Clematis vitalba, **Clematis**

Clematis is a prolific and tangled vine which supports itself by covering trees. Preferring to grow high up, it hangs about as a soft and misty mass. So it is for the Clematis type whose mind floats about, softly and dreamily, with very little structure in life.

Fagus sylvatica, **Beech**

No other shrubs or trees are tolerated in a Beech wood and Beech leaves are hard and shiny. Thus the Beech type is unable to tolerate others and may become hardened and critical.

Gentianella amarella, **Gentian**

From the high places where the late-flowering autumn Gentian grows, it is easier to see life from a broader viewpoint. This helps the Gentian type to feel less discouraged and understand it is never too late to find a new perspective on life.

Helianthemum nummularium, **Rock Rose**

Great fear can leave the Rock Rose type almost paralyzed, or frozen, but just as the sun melts ice, this yellow, sun-like flower essence can warm and re-activate the system.

Hottonia palustris, **Water Violet**

The Water Violet likes to grow in deep inaccessible dykes, reflecting the Water Violet type who prefers to withdraw from life.

Ilex aquifoliaceae, **Holly**

The Holly, with its prickly leaves, is the tree of Christmas, with a strong tradition of warding off evil. Thus it can protect the Holly type from the powerful and prickly negativity that attacks from within and so renew the heart with love.

Impatiens glandulifera, **Impatiens**

The seed pods of the quick-growing Impatiens plant explode like bullets, just as the Impatiens type flares up with impatience.

Juglans regia, **Walnut**

The Walnut has a subtle fragrance that keeps birds, insects and other plants at bay, and as a flower essence Walnut gives protection from any negative outside influences.

Larix decidua, **Larch**

The delicate branches of the Larch droop, seemingly lacking the strength to stand erect, and the Larch type lacks the confidence to try new things.

Lonicera caprifolium, **Honeysuckle**

The sweet fragrance of the Honeysuckle, as with many strong scents, can bring back strong recollections of the past, reflecting the Honeysuckle type's preoccupation with the past.

△ **Crab Apple**

Malus sylvestris, **Crab Apple**

Cutting open an apple reveals a five-pointed star, which is the symbol of immortality: reflecting this, the Crab Apple type becomes able to see life in its true perspective.

△ **Honeysuckle**

△ Mimulus

△ Olive

Mimulus guttatus, Mimulus

Inherent in this flower is a huge courage as it can choose to live precariously, hanging from a bank half in the water. Its roots go down deep, so it knows it is safe. Mimulus types find similar courage, as this essence makes them aware of the strength and safety deep within themselves.

Olea europaea, Olive

The Olive tree fruits even when bent with age. So Olive types will give until their reserves are totally depleted. Nevertheless, the Olive tree is inexhaustible and will regenerate from an old stump, and the essence can renew the energy and strength of an exhausted person.

Ornithogalum umbellatum, Star of Bethlehem

The Star of Bethlehem has a perfectly symmetrical six-pointed flower, giving the message that it can rebalance the system of an individual, which may have become misaligned after a trauma.

Pinus sylvestris, Pine

The Pine tree's sap has sharp, cleansing properties, and it is known for its purifying qualities. Consequently this essence can purify the Pine type's unhealthy thought patterns.

Populus tremula, Aspen

Aspen leaves tremble even when there is not a breath of wind, and the Aspen type shakes and quivers with fear for no apparent reason. The tree is a type of poplar.

Prunus cerasifera, Cherry Plum

Blooming when the countryside is still in the grip of winter storms, this is the first blossom of the year. White, pure and fresh, it is a reminder that spring is just around the corner, and will bring an end to the dark storms in the mind of the Cherry Plum type.

Quercus robur, Oak

The Oak tree gives sustenance to countless other creatures, so the Oak type helps others and shoulders great burdens of work and responsibility.

"What right have you, O passer-by-the-way, to call any flower a weed? Do you know its merits, virtues, healing qualities? Because a thing is common, shall you despise it? If so, you might as well despise the sun for the same reason."

Anon

△ Cherry Plum

△ Oak

The Oak tree will struggle into leaf no matter how old or decayed it has become, and the Oak type can also break down or fall ill from overwork, but will still attempt to carry on.

Rosa canina, **Wild Rose**

The Wild Rose is also known as the Dog Rose because the thorns have some resemblance to a dog's claw. It is useful to remember how enthusiastic dogs are, very different from the apathy and resignation of the Wild Rose type.

Salix vitellina, **Willow**

The Willow grows in wet, stagnant, muddy and often smelly places where other trees would quickly rot; this mirrors the chronic resentment and bitterness of the Willow type, a state that can persist for years.

△ Wild Rose

△ Mustard

Scleranthus annus, **Scleranthus**

Scleranthus has many tangled stems growing in all directions, which reflects the inner confusion of this type of person. Sensitive to the environment, it is here today and gone tomorrow, reflecting the Scleranthus type's changeable heart.

Sinapis arvensis, **Mustard**

The Mustard plant appears suddenly on seemingly bare land, an expanse of glowing yellow flowers, which brightens and cheers the mind of the depressed Mustard type.

Ulex europaeus, **Gorse**

The Gorse flowers throughout the dark and cold of winter, encouraging the Gorse type to let in the sunshine of hope, even when things seem most dark and dire.

Ulmus procera, **Elm**

Even the magnificent Elm can be laid low by a tiny fungus just as even the most strong and responsible of people can suddenly feel unable to cope with their circumstances. Since the Elm can quickly regenerate, this depressed state can prove temporary for the Elm type.

Verbena officinalis, **Vervain**

The tangled stems of the Vervain reflect the busyness of the stressed person. Its flowers are tiny, the plant having put in a lot of effort to achieve relatively little. As a result the Vervain type will strain and strive to get things done and often gets life quite out of proportion.

Vitis vinifera, **Vine**

The Vine uses its tendrils to grip on to whatever it can reach for support and a means of growing. This reflects Vine types who use others for their own ends, because they feel weak and unable to support themselves on an inner level.

Rock Water

This is not strictly a flower essence but is water that is collected from a natural spring. Just as water eventually wears away stone, so this essence can dissolve the hardness or resistence in Rock Water types and, like water, they can learn to flow with life.

△ Vervain

The Flower Essences

"Flowers are conscious, intelligent forces. They have been given to us for our happiness and healing."

Lila Devi. Masters Flower Essences

Understanding the Bach essences

Flower essence therapy as we know it today began with the Bach flower essences. Fitting together like a jigsaw puzzle, the 38 emotional states the essences address are said to cover the human condition on the personality level. Tried and tested world-wide, the Bach system provides emotional support for people, animals and plants with physical complaints, and also for those who are healthy but suffer from mental and emotional stress. The essences are chosen according to how a person feels about their difficulty, a process that is not invasive. The compactness of the Bach set make it a good starting point for people who are beginning their journey into flower essences.

the Twelve Healers

The essences in the first group that Dr Bach prepared are all sun potentized and are essences that heal the personality and bring harmony to the soul, mind and body connection. From birth onwards, life experiences accumulate, like the layers of an onion, to create the person of today, while deep within, the essential loving self remains unchangeable and naturally perfect. The personality embodies the lessons of life and its negative expression shows where growth is needed.

◁ Treasure your essences and keep them in a specially designed box. The separate compartments keep their individual healing properties clear.

▷ Each stock will yield up to 100 dosage bottles. A little goes a long way, and only an occasional bottle will need replacing.

The Twelve Healers are called "type" essences and support the personality to develop virtues and find balance. It is therefore of enormous value to discover your main essence (or group of essences, as often a combination of two or three can be indicated).

When life gets difficult, your behaviour usually has a predictable pattern to it. This is contained in the personality picture of the type essence or combination. For example, Scleranthus types can sometimes become unfocused, changeable, and find it difficult to

◁ Flower essences can gently strip away the constricting and unresolved layers of the "personality onion", to reveal our true potential.

THE TWELVE HEALERS

Failing	Essence	Virtue
Restraint	Chicory	Love
Fear	Mimulus	Sympathy
Restlessness	Agrimony	Peace
Indecision	Scleranthus	Steadfastness
Indifference	Clematis	Gentleness
Weakness	Centaury	Strength
Doubt	Gentian	Understanding
Over-enthusiasm	Vervain	Tolerance
Ignorance	Cerato	Wisdom
Impatience	Impatiens	Forgiveness
Terror	Rock Rose	Courage
Grief	Water Violet	Joy

the New Nineteen Essences

The New Nineteen Essences are prepared using the boiling method, with the exception of White Chestnut. The mental and emotional states they address "grow out" of those associated with the Twelve Healers and Seven Helpers, being more extreme and diverse expressions of these states. The Nineteen Essences are not for the personality self, but are designed to develop spiritual or soul qualities, and to give protection from the influences of others. They are also helpful in clearing the layers of the "personality onion", so it is often necessary to use some of the New Nineteen to allow the Healers and Helpers to work effectively.

THE NEW NINETEEN ESSENCES

Aspen
Beech
Cherry Plum
Chestnut Bud
Crab Apple
Elm
Holly
Honeysuckle
Hornbeam
Larch
Mustard
Pine
Red Chestnut
Star of Bethlehem
Sweet Chestnut
Walnut
White Chestnut
Wild Rose
Willow

make a decision, while Impatiens types can become impatient and hot-tempered. It can be useful to take a type essence during periods of stress, no matter what other essences are indicated, as it can help you to function more positively and effectively.

the Twelve Healers as the lessons of life

Dr Bach described the Twelve Healers as the twelve great lessons of life, and recommended that the inherent failing should not be repressed, as this gives it more power, but that it can be washed away by developing the opposing virtue. Although you may be working on some of these difficulties in particular, all twelve moods can be applicable to everyone at one time or another.

the Seven Helpers

The Seven Helpers are particularly useful for chronic states as these can run so deep that they seem to be part of the essential self, but in truth are not. Similar to a type essence these essences are also sun potentized, and it is useful to see which of the seven seem most appropriate to you as they can prove helpful if the healers are not fully effective. Emotional states can be reflected in the complexion, so try Vine, Heather or Rock Water if you have a high colour, or Olive, Gorse or Oak if you are pale. If none of these six seem right, try Wild Oat. With the Twelve Healers, the Seven Helpers complete the first half of the set.

THE SEVEN HELPERS

Gorse
Heather
Oak
Olive
Rock Water
Vine
Wild Oat

Holly and Wild Oat – the openers

If you are treating someone for the first time, it may be that they seem to require a very large number of essences. If this is the case Holly and Wild Oat are used as initial treatments to open up the person and help the true nature of the problem to become clear. You should give Holly essence if the individual seems extrovert, or Wild Oat essence if they seem introvert. Over the subsequent treatment sessions the client should become more open, and their difficulties more clearly seen, and you will find it easy to diagnose an appropriate essence.

The seven groupings of the Bach essences

Bach broke down human personalites, with their mental and emotional aspects, into seven groups. Within each group, or classification, he described a number of behavioural variations, which he believed covered all personality states known to humanity. These variations total 38, and he discovered a flower essence that would counter each of them.

The seven groups are: fear; uncertainty; insufficient interest in present circumstances; loneliness; over-sensitive to ideas and influences; despondency or despair; over-care for the welfare of others. Bach's essences are then placed within these seven groups and between them they cover the basic areas of emotional difficulty the human condition presents.

the fear group

Aesculus x carnea, Red Chestnut
Flowers in early summer. Pick flowering twigs, including leaves. Boiling method.

the Red Chestnut temperament
Red Chestnut types worry excessively over the safety of their loved ones, which may cause them considerable distress. They often project situations, usually imagining the worst, and prove over-protective. The Red Chestnut essence can bring forth the ability to "let go" of loved ones without feeling fear; it becomes possible to trust that they will be "looked after".

affirmations
• I am radiating peace and calm from within myself.

• I am letting my loved ones go, trusting that they are in safe hands.

indications for using Red Chestnut
• For those who imagine the worst when a loved one is late home.
• For those who try to manipulate or control their loved ones through over-caring.
• For those who worry over the health of a loved one.

keywords
Negative Over-concern, smothering, over-protectiveness, over-attachment.
Positive Trust, optimistic outlook, positive thinking.

Helianthemum nummularium, Rock Rose
Flowers in summer. Pick individual flowers. Sun potentized.

the Rock Rose temperament
Rock Rose types are extremely open and sensitive individuals and can suffer deep fears, usually on unseen levels that are difficult to penetrate. Often drawn to a life of service to others, these people are capable of great self-sacrifice and, in times of hardship, of superhuman courage. Rock Rose essence is ideal for people who suffer from nightmares or who are taking drugs, and is indicated whenever there is great terror or panic. It is an ingredient in all rescue or emergency formulas.

affirmations
• I am filling up with courage and strength.
• I have the fearlessness of a lion.
• I can access superhuman courage.

indications for using Rock Rose
• For those with blank and staring eyes.
• For those who easily lose control and become hysterical.
• For those who become paralysed with fear and may be unable to act.
• For those with a drug problem.

keywords
Negative Alarm, fear, terror, panic, nightmares, numbness.
Positive Courage, strength, self-sacrifice, unshakable, conviction.

△ Red Chestnut: excessive fear for other people.

△ Rock Rose: extreme fear or panic.

Mimulus guttatus, Mimulus

Flowers in summer. Pick individual flowers. Sun potentized.

the Mimulus temperament

Mimulus types are shy, timid and reserved. They are sensitive and find life frightening but keep their fears private. They are often nervous and afraid to be alone. Mimulus is the essence for phobias, such as fear of spiders, the dark, heights or knives. This essence can bring forth the expression of courage, strength and understanding, but without the loss of sensitivity.

affirmations

• My fears are diminishing, I am free.
• I am letting go of the limits of fear.

indications for using Mimulus

• For a child who seems reluctant to join in games with other children.
• Supportive in cases of vertigo, agoraphobia and other phobias.
• For those who tend to blush, have a stammer, or whose hands become clammy with fear.
• Mimulus with Aspen can be used to cover both of the fear types, known and unknown.

keywords

Negative Phobias, timidity, nervousness, shyness, anxieties.
Positive Courage, safety, security.

△ **Mimulus: for known fears.**

△ **Aspen: fears of an unknown origin.**

Populus tremula, Aspen

Flowers in early spring. Pick male and female catkins on flowering twigs. Boiling method.

the Aspen temperament

Aspen types can have unexpected panic or anxiety attacks. There appears to be no apparent reason for this reaction and it becomes quite difficult to cope with. There may be trembling, delusions, nightmares and fear of all things evil, and the imagination can run riot. This essence can bring forth feelings of great inner strength and security, so fear can find no place.

affirmations

• My aura is open to only joy and light.
• I am protected by the light.
• I am in safe hands.

indications for using Aspen

• For those who wake with a sense of foreboding.
• For fear of the dark.
• For panic attacks, use with Honeysuckle essence to dissolve the original fearful memory.

keywords

Negative Trembling, apprehension, hypersensitivity, shakiness.
Positive Openness, fearlessness, courage.

Prunus cerasifera, Cherry Plum

Flowers in early spring. Pick flowering twigs, avoiding leaves. Boiling method.

the Cherry Plum temperament

Cherry Plum types may have fearful thoughts and irrational, uncontrolled outbreaks of temper; with a fear of doing things they do not really want to do and consequently find it difficult to "let go" of a current situation. Cherry Plum essence can bring the ability to control behaviour and give a renewed connection to inner strength. Serenity and inner peace can grow while learning to live more spontaneously and with greater confidence.

affirmations

• I accept my inner guidance.
• I can let go and let peace in.
• My energy is balanced, I can relax.

indications for using Cherry Plum

• For a child who wets the bed.
• For those who experience extreme tension, and may have an uncontrollable temper.

keywords

Negative Irrational, suicidal, nervous breakdown, uncontrolled delusions, abusive, hysterical.
Positive Calm, stable, spontaneous, self-control, inner connection, resilience, openess to change.

△ **Cherry Plum: fear of losing control.**

the uncertainty group

△ **Wild Oat: a lack of direction in life.**

Bromus ramosus, Wild Oat

Flowers in summer. Pick flowering heads. Sun potentized.

the Wild Oat temperament

Wild Oat types may seem bored and aimless, they can become depressed when things in their life do not seem clear. They possess many talents and will have tried several different occupations but cannot commit to one and find permanency, and this brings dissatisfaction with all areas of their life. Wild Oat essence can bring an insight into what the right life path is, and what, if anything, might be blocking a commitment to it.

affirmations

• Day by day my true life plan is clearer.
• I am hearing the guidance of my soul.

indications for using Wild Oat

• For those who have had many different occupations, none of which seemed right.
• For those who don't seem to know what they want.
• For the introvert type who seems to need all the essences, Wild Oat is ideal.

keywords

Negative Dithering, aimless, frustrated, uncertain, dissatisfied, bored.
Positive Vision, choice, direction, strength, purpose, focus, commitment, true realization.

Carpinus betulus, Hornbeam

Flowers in late spring. Pick flowering twigs with male and female catkins. Boiling method.

the Hornbeam temperament

Hornbeam types wake heavy-headed, tired and disinclined to face yet another grey day. However, if something interesting happens they come to life! It is a mental attitude to the things they have to do that makes them feel tired and disinterested. Hornbeam essence can bring forth the expression of a cool clear head, revitalize the mind and give the enthusiasm to cope with all the tasks required.

affirmations

• I feel awake and refreshed.
• I am interested in everything I do.
• I can find the fun in everything I do.

indications for using Hornbeam

• For those who feel they do not have the strength to do normal activities.
• For those who are living a life with too much cerebral work.
• For those whose life is in a rut, this essence can help make a change.

keywords

Negative Mental tiredness, procrastination, heaviness, disinterestedness.
Positive Clarity, resilience, strength, coolness, enthusiasm.

△ **Hornbeam: Monday morning feelings.**

△ **Cerato: lack of confidence in your own judgement.**

Ceratostigma willmottianum, Cerato

Flowers in early autumn. Pick individual flowers. Sun potentized.

the Cerato temperament

Cerato types mistrust their own decisions and often feel the need to ask for advice. They can appear gullible, in need of approval and lacking in concentration. Their identity seems weak and they often follow the latest trends. Cerato essence can bring forth trust in the "inner voice". With increased belief in a sense of judgement comes the ability to act wisely and with conviction. There is renewed enthusiasm for life and an eagerness to learn.

affirmations

• I trust my inner voice.
• My intuition is strong and true.
• My intuition will guide me to my highest will.

indications for using Cerato

• For those who have made a decision, but then feel the need to talk it over with friends.
• For those who feel undermined by other's differing opinions.
• For the adolescent who is following the crowd or the latest cult.
• For those who ask advice, but never seem to act on it.

- For those who always do the "right thing", rather than what they want.

keywords
Negative Uncertainty, foolishness, seeking approval and reassurance.
Positive Self-trust, confidence, intuition, uninfluenced, strong convictions.

Gentianella amarella, Gentian
Flowers in early autumn. Pick individual flowers. Sun potentized.

the Gentian temperament
Gentian types almost enjoy their negativity and "wouldn't be happy even if they were". They lack faith, are pessimistic and may have lost their spiritual connection. Easily discouraged by set-backs, they feel depressed and disheartened but always know why. Gentian essence can bring forth a positive more optimistic approach to life. It kindles the feeling that their best really is good enough.

affirmations
- I am finding deeper meaning in life.
- I can see life with renewed optimism.
- My best is always good enough.
- I will learn to view the positive side.

indications for using Gentian
- For those who get depressed when things go wrong.

△ **Gentian: feelings of depression and pessimism.**

△ **Scleranthus: indecision, first one thing seems right, then the other.**

- For those who have failed a driving test, yet again.
- For set-backs during illness, to regain the lost ground more quickly.

keywords
Negative Pessimistic, discouraged, negative, depressed, sceptical, disheartened.
Positive Faith, optimism, perseverance, conviction, cheerful, positive.

Scleranthus annus, Scleranthus
Flowers in summer. Pick flowering sprigs. Sun potentized.

the Scleranthus temperament
Scleranthus types cannot make up their minds, vacillating first one way, then the other, often over trivial matters. They rarely ask for advice, preferring patiently to make up their own minds. Lacking inner balance, their moods fluctuate and they may appear fickle or confused. Scleranthus essence can bring forth balance and the ability to make the right decision at the right time.

affirmations
- My inner self speaks with clarity, it is easy to know what to do next.
- My mind is focused as the days pass.

indications for using Scleranthus
- For those who suffer from travel sickness.
- For those who find it difficult to decide on what to choose.

- For those who have difficulty keeping their balance.

keywords
Negative Indecision, vacillation, uncertainty, confusion, mood swings.
Positive Balance, stability, decisiveness, harmony, clarity.

Ulex europaeus, Gorse
Flowers in spring, Pick individual flowers. Sun potentized.

the Gorse temperament
Gorse types often have chronic complaints and may feel utterly hopeless. They can lose all hope of improvement, feeling there is no point in trying, and may acquire an air of resignation. Full of despair, they are usually pale and lack energy. Gorse essence can bring forth the expression of positive acceptance, enabling them to see the bright side of life and find renewed hope.

affirmations
- Every day is a new day.
- I live each day with renewed hope.

indications for using Gorse
- For those who feel there is no point in seeking further help for a complaint.
- For those who have had disappointing failures and refuse to try again.

keywords
Negative Resigned, negative, despairing, suffering, hopeless.
Positive Faith, hope, insight, acceptance.

△ **Gorse: chronic feelings of hopelessness.**

the insufficient interest in present circumstances group

Aesculus hippocastanum, Chestnut Bud

Flowers in late spring. Pick both male and female flowers still on the twigs. Boiling method.

the Chestnut Bud temperament

Chestnut Bud types can be very slow to learn due to a lack of interest or observation. They fail to learn from their mistakes through inner haste, indifference, mental blocks or retarded development. The Chestnut Bud essence brings forth mental flexibility which helps people to become more reflective, to learn and to keep their attention focused in the present.

affirmations

- I am switched on to life.
- I am learning from every new experience.
- I know the joy of learning.

indications for using Chestnut Bud

- For those who repeat the same patterns.
- For the child who forgets something routine, such as their lunch box, again and again.
- In cases where an essence has not

△ **Chestnut Bud: repeating the same mistakes.**

△ **White Chestnut: unwanted and worrying thoughts.**

been effective, try a different approach, including this essence.

- For those who get a number of complaints repeatedly at the same time of the year.

keywords

Negative Indifference, slow learner, forgetful, lack of observation, fixations. *Positive* Attentive, present, reflective, always learning, observant.

Aesculus hippocastanum, White Chestnut

Flowers in early summer. Pick individual flowers. Sun potentized.

the White Chestnut temperament

White Chestnut types have over-active minds and are plagued with uncontrollable thoughts going round and round in the head. Such incessant mental chatter can make the head feel full and headachy and may cause a lack of concentration or sleep. White Chestnut essence can bring forth a balanced mind with a clear, calm head, becoming more able to focus and think methodically and constructively.

affirmations

- My head is a peaceful place.
- My mind is gently filling with quiet and calm.

Indications for using White Chestnut

- For those who worry all the time.
- For those who cannot stop thinking about something.
- When a snippet of a song is going round and round in the head.
- For those who go over and over earlier conversations, thinking about what they might have said.

keywords

Negative Worrying thoughts, mental chatter, over-active mind, exhaustion. *Positive* Peace, calm, concentration, solutions, focus, clarity.

Clematis vitalba, Clematis

Flowers in summer. Pick individual blooms. Sun potentized.

the Clematis temperament

Clematis types appear bored and empty-headed, as their thoughts are usually elsewhere. They have very little interest in life, a poor memory and may need a lot of sleep. Lacking vitality and usually pale, they can appear vague and spaced-out, and they are often very idealistic or impractical. The Clematis essence brings forth the expression of a renewed interest in life and assists thoughts to become more focused and realistic. It is often indicated for artistic people, who will consequently find themselves becoming more productive.

"Some people dream of success while others work hard at it."

Anon

△ **Clematis: for daydreamers who have little interest in life**.

affirmations
• I am wide awake, alert and here.
• I am happy to live in the present.
• My creative talents and thoughts are blossoming.

indications for using Clematis
• For those who are forgetful or always bumping into things.
• For those trying to release their creative powers and are in need of some inspiration.
• For those who like to daydream and spend too much time living in a fantasy world.
• For the child who spends most of school time gazing out of the classroom window.
• Helpful for women before the start of their menstruation.
• For those who have amazing ideas, but then take no action to make things happen.

keywords
Negative Daydreaming, inattentive, bored, sleepy, impractical, absentminded, ungrounded.
Positive Purpose, meaning, focused, creative, interested, productive, earthed.

"Our greatest glory is not in never failing, but in rising up every time we fail."

Ralph Waldo Emerson

Lonicera caprifolium, Honeysuckle
Flowers in early summer. Pick flowering stems. Boiling method.

the Honeysuckle temperament
The Honeysuckle type is unable to forget their past; tending to be wistful and nostalgic, they glorify the past and yearn to be there – perhaps with long-lost loved ones or simply just back in what they are sure were "the good old days". Honeysuckle essence may be

△ **Honeysuckle: living in the past**.

given to release troublesome, unhappy memories, for instance in cases of bereavement, or to comfort chronic homesickness. This essence can bring forth the ability to learn from past experiences, and then to let them go. Honeysuckle helps people to live in the present with interest and enthusiasm, and with a forward-looking attitude.

affirmations
• Life is always changing.
• I am happy to live in the present.
• Present time is where I want to be.

indications for using Honeysuckle
• For homesickness, for those who are going away to school or college, or moving house.
• For those who are unable to make plans for the future.
• If there are difficulties in resolving a phobia, add Honeysuckle essence to a combination to help dissolve the memory of the original traumatic event and help to release any fear in the present.

keywords
Negative Nostalgia, homesickness, wistfulness, longing, regrets.
Positive Interest, liveliness, energy, living in the present.

▷

Olea europaea, Olive

Flowers in early summer. Pick flowering sprays, avoiding leaves. Sun potentized.

The Olive temperament

Olive types feel complete mental and physical tiredness, which can develop after illness or a period of prolonged strain or overwork. They have no reserves of strength left and everything becomes an overwhelming effort, even activities they normally enjoy. The Olive essence can bring forth renewed energy and vitality and is ideal in very acute conditions.

affirmations

- I am able to take care of myself.
- I feel my energy is renewed and rejuvenated.
- I have all the strength I need for all I have to do.

Indications for using Olive

- For those who have no strength left to make an effort.
- For mothers during childbirth, breast-feeding or sleepless nights.
- Ideal for support during convalescence.

keywords

Negative Tired, weary, exhausted, overworked, drained, sapped, ordeal.
Positive Vitality, strength, energy.

△ **Olive: complete mental and physical exhaustion.**

△ **Wild Rose: resignation and apathy.**

Rosa canina, Wild Rose

Flowers in summer. Pick flowering twigs. Boiling method.

the Wild Rose temperament

Wild Rose types may be sad, indifferent, lack vitality and feel easily bored, because they are not interested in anything. Totally resigned, they never complain, as they consider this state normal, and they have given up all efforts to improve their life. The Wild Rose essence can bring forth a renewed interest and zest for life.

affirmations

- I notice life becoming more interesting day by day.
- I feel very alert, I am involving myself totally in life.

indications for using Wild Rose

- For those who accept a mind-numbing daily routine and have no interest or joy in life.
- For those who seem entirely apathetic and do not care what happens to them in life.
- For those who have felt like giving up on life.

keywords

Negative Resignation, apathy, boredom, indifference, joylessness.
Positive Vitality, interest, enjoyment, alertness, zest.

Sinapsis arvensis, Mustard

Flowers in summer. Pick flowering sprays, avoiding leaves. Boiling method.

the Mustard temperament

Mustard types suffer from black depression and gloom. It descends like a dark cloud and may last days or weeks. Mustard types are afraid of such gloom because they feel powerless and find it impossible to disguise. The Mustard essence can bring forth serenity, cheerfulness and a stable lighter mood.

affirmations

- Sunny cheerfulness always comes easily to me.
- I am happy whatever the weather.
- I am standing in the light.

Indications for using Mustard

- For adolescents who are frequently miserable and moody for no reason.
- For those who suffer from depressive symptoms for no reason.
- For those who may find their gloom or general melancholia is affected by the weather.

keywords

Negative Melancholia, gloom, black depression, powerlessness.
Positive Cheerfulness, stability, lightness, inner serenity.

△ **Mustard: cycles of deep gloom due to an unknown cause.**

the loneliness group

Calluna vulgaris, Heather

Flowers in late summer. Pick tips of flowering sprigs. Sun potentized.

the Heather temperament

Heather types are self-centred. They exaggerate their problems and need to be the centre of attention. Unhappy if they have to be alone, they talk constantly about themselves and are poor listeners. Consequently the Heather types are not popular, as people find their presence is tiring and they prove difficult to get away from. The Heather essence brings forth comfort, confidence, and turns this type into a better listener.

affirmations

- It is easy to listen.
- What I need is coming to me.
- I concentrate on the good in my life.

indications for using Heather

- For those who continually bring the conversation back to themselves.
- For those who are ready to relate their complete life history to a stranger.
- For those who need their symptoms to get attention.

keywords

Negative Lonely, self-centred, poor listener, demanding, self-obsessed.
Positive Empathic, sympathetic, caring, listening, objective.

△ **Heather: obsessed with personal troubles.**

△ **Water Violet: feelings of superiority.**

Hottonia palustris, Water Violet

Flowers in early summer. Pick individual flowers. Sun potentized.

the Water Violet temperament

Water Violet types show little emotional involvement in life and keep to themselves. They never interfere in other people's affairs and are thought to be conceited and unreachable. Preferring isolation, they often attempt to withdraw from life completely. This essence can bring a reconnection with life and people, allowing Water Violet types to enjoy sharing their many healing gifts.

affirmations

- I am joyfully involving myself with all aspects of life.
- It is easy to connect with others.

indications for using Water Violet

- For the overly self-reliant individual, who prefers to be alone.
- For those who make their home an impregnable castle.

keywords

Negative Aloofness, superiority, isolation, conceited, reserved, condescending.
Positive Humility, wisdom, service, balance, love, warmth.

Impatiens glandulifera, Impatiens

Flowers in summer and autumn. Pick the pale mauve flowers only. Sun potentized.

the Impatiens temperament

Impatiens types get frustrated if things do not go fast enough. They prefer to work alone, as other people make them feel impatient. Hot-tempered, they flare up easily, but it is quickly over, at least for them. Suffering from extreme inner tension, they may get nervous indigestion, hot flushes and sudden pains, or they can be accident-prone. The Impatiens essence can bring forth patience and understanding of others, calmness and diplomacy.

affirmations

- Calm and patience come easily to me.
- I understand that everyone has their own pace of life.

Indications for using Impatiens

- For those who tend to finish other people's sentences.
- For fidgeting, squabbling children.
- For those who start projects but fail to finish them.

keywords

Negative Impatience, irritability, frustration, quick temper, fidgeting.
Positive Patience, empathy, tolerance, understanding.

△ **Impatiens: impatience with others.**

the over-sensitive to influences and ideas group

Agrimonia eupatoria, Agrimony

Flowers in summer. Pick tips of
flowering spikes. Sun potentized.

the Agrimony temperament

Agrimony types hide behind a mask of
cheerfulness and find it hard to
communicate their feelings. They can
be deeply distressed by conflict. They may
overwork or use alcohol or drugs. The
Agrimony essence brings peace and calm,
making it easier to express feelings.

affirmations

• I am finding peace within myself.
• I can safely express my feelings.

indications for using Agrimony

• For those who wake up at night,
 feeling restless.
• For those who make light of things
 and laugh when they want to cry.

keywords

Negative Restless, addiction, loneliness.
Positive Peace, honesty, expressiveness.

Centaurium umbellatum, Centaury

Flowers in summer and autumn. Pick
individual flowers. Sun potentized.

the Centaury temperament

Centaury types are timid and submissive,
and are often dominated by others. They
work beyond their strength, and may
appear weak, pale and tired. Centaury can
bring the strength to be more assertive.

△ **Centaury: weak, easily dominated personality.**

affirmations

• I am standing up for myself.
• I am clear about my boundaries.
• I am living an independent life.

indications for using Centaury

• For those who feel the need to take
 care of others.
• For the victims of bullying.
• Co-dependent types who give away
 their power.

keywords

Negative Weakness, submissiveness.
Positive Assertiveness, individuality, will,
strength, boundaries.

Ilex aquifolium, Holly

Flowers in early summer. Pick flowering
twigs. Boiling method.

the Holly temperament

Holly types are hard-hearted, angry,
jealous and suspicious. Super-sensitive and
mistrusting, they are unhappy but, sadly, do
not always know why. The Holly essence
can bring forth the expression of love,
forgiveness and understanding.

affirmations

• I am opening my heart to love.
• Everything is as it should be.

indications for using Holly

• For those who envy others they feel are
 happier than themselves.
• For children or animals who may be
 jealous of a new addition to the family.

keywords

Negative Jealousy, mistrust, envy.
Positive Love, forgiveness, generosity.

Juglans regia, Walnut

Flowers in late spring. Pick twigs with
male and female flowers. Boiling method.

the Walnut temperament

Walnut is indicated during the
transitional phases of life, and supports
the "letting go" of things. This essence
can bring forth a feeling of protection
and helps clarity of thought.

affirmations

• I feel safe and protected.
• I can move through life uninfluenced.

indications for using Walnut:

• For those who are affected by negative
 surroundings.
• For those who resist change.

keywords

Negative Vulnerable, held back, resistant.
Positive Flexibility, freedom, protection,
acceptance, adjusting, moving on.

△ **Agrimony: inner torture behind a brave face.**

△ **Holly: strong feelings.**

△ **Walnut: protection, breaking with the past.**

the despair and despondency group

△ **Sweet Chestnut: extreme despair and despondency.**

Castanea sativa, Sweet Chestnut

Flowers in summer. Pick twigs bearing male and female flowers. Boiling method.

the Sweet Chestnut temperament

Sweet Chestnut types frequently experience that "back-to-the-wall" feeling. Having reached their deepest states of despondency and despair, all hope is abandoned and it feels like "the dark night of the soul". In this extreme state the Sweet Chestnut essence can bring forth feelings of comfort, and the return of faith. Feelings of renewal and inner transformation may take place.

affirmations
- My inner core feels comforted.
- Beyond the darkness I can experience the light.

indications for using Sweet Chestnut
- For those that feel the anguish of life is too much to be endured.
- For those who reach the utmost limits of their strength.
- For those who need comfort after a close bereavement.

keywords
Negative Despair, despondency, anguish, limits of endurance.
Positive Hope, new inner life, spiritual renewal, faith.

Larix decidua, Larch

Flowers in spring. Pick twigs with male and female blooms. Boiling method.

the Larch temperament

Larch types believe themselves to be inferior and lack the confidence to do the activities they see others doing. They display an air of "false modesty" and, expecting to fail at things, never even try, their internal message being "I can't". They can appear self-effacing, passive and lacking in determination. The Larch essence can bring forth the expression of objectivity and perseverance. With each new small success, self-confidence grows.

affirmations
- I have the confidence to try new things and succeed.
- I am as capable as everyone else.

indications for using Larch
- Larch is helpful for everyone at one time or another.
- For those who believe everyone is better "qualified" than they are.
- For those who may fear failure.

keywords
Negative Lack of confidence, inferiority, false modesty, failure.
Positive Capable, determined, confident, perseverance, focus.

△ **Larch: feelings of inferiority and lack of confidence.**

△ **Crab Apple: for those who feel self-disgust and may become obsessive.**

Malus sylvestris, Crab Apple

Flowers in late spring. Pick flowering twigs. Boiling method.

the Crab Apple temperament

This is the essence for cleansing and eliminating toxicity on all levels. Crab Apple types can feel deep self-disgust or shame. They can become obsessional and have fixations: they may think their nose is too big, for instance, or feel dirty over some act and have to wash every five minutes. The Crab Apple essence is helpful for seeing life in its true perspective.

affirmations
- I am perfect just as I am.
- I can see things in their true perspective.

indications for using Crab Apple
- When there is a need for physical cleansing, as in cases of skin problems or spots.
- For those who feel disgust at normal everyday physical contact.
- For those who can feel contaminated.
- For those who are preoccupied with changing their appearance.

keywords
Negative Impure, disgust, infected, revolted, obsessed, compulsive.
Positive Purity, innocence, perspective, self-respect, self-love.

▷

Ornithogalum umbellatum, Star of Bethlehem

Flowers in late spring. Pick flowering stems. Boiling method.

the Star of Bethlehem temperament

Star of Bethlehem types have often had shocking experiences, the effects of which can still be felt years later. Should the body's life-force be blocked by shock, the natural healing processes will find it difficult to function. This essence can release the body's healing energies, allowing them to work more effectively. Star of Bethlehem is known as the comforter and soother of sorrow.

affirmations

- It is easy to let go of past pains.
- All my levels are vibrating in perfect harmony.

indications for using Star of Bethlehem

- For those who cannot get over a loss.
- For those who cannot be comforted and are unable to cry.
- This is a helpful essence to add to the first treatment bottle

keywords

Negative Mental numbness, shock, trauma, bemusement, grief.
Positive Peace, comfort, equilibrium, balance, healing.

△ **Star of Bethlehem: after-effects of physical, mental and emotional shock.**

△ **Pine: guilt and unworthy feelings.**

Pinus sylvestris, Pine

Flowers in early summer. Pick male and female flowers. Boiling method.

the Pine temperament

Pine types are of an apologetic and introverted nature. They feel responsible for the mistakes of others and have high expectations of themselves. These people find it difficult to accept anything (including love), as their self-esteem is so low. With such deep feelings of unworthiness they may unconsciously seek self-punishment. This essence can bring forth the expression of inner forgiveness, self-worth and strength. Those needing Pine can begin to admit their faults with compassion for themselves and to have genuine regret rather than guilt.

affirmations

- I approve of myself exactly as I am.
- I am born perfect and I am now remembering my true essence.
- I forgive myself for believing that I need to be forgiven.

indications for using Pine

- For those who feel they could have done better.
- For those who are always saying sorry when it is not their fault.

keywords

Negative Self-reproach, guilt, apologizing, self-blame, perfectionism.

Positive Self-forgiveness, genuine regret, understanding, balance.

Quercus robur, Oak

Flowers in late spring. Pick tiny red female flowers only. Sun potentized.

the Oak temperament

Oak types are dutiful, reliable plodders, serious and over-responsible. They have superhuman endurance and patience, never giving up or complaining in the face of overwhelming odds. Often hiding their growing exhaustion, they can have unexpected breakdowns of mental and/or physical health. The Oak essence can bring forth flexibility and resistance to stress. They learn to delegate and begin to use their energies in a balanced way.

affirmations

- I am finding my limits.
- I can relax and let go of struggle.

indications for using Oak

- For those who neglect their own needs.
- For those whose life seems all duty.
- For those who carry on, even when there is no hope of winning.

keywords

Negative Over-effort, over-conscientiousness, seriousness, burden, despair.
Positive Strong, balanced, playful, flexible, brave, faithful.

△ **Oak: for those who never give up.**

△ **Willow: unspoken resentment, a life that seems unfair.**

"Worry never robs tomorrow of its sorrow, it only saps today of its joy."

Leo Buscaglia

Salix vitellina, Willow

Flowers in late spring. Pick twigs bearing male and female flowers. Boiling method.

the Willow temperament

Willow types blame everyone else for their situation and feel life to be unfair. They can be negative, moody, and have bitter, spiteful thoughts. They may be sulky, or have a "poor me" attitude, seeing themselves as victims of fate. This essence can bring an understanding of personal power, responsibility and the importance of a positive and humorous attitude to life.

affirmations

• I am taking total responsibility for my own actions.
• I am radiating positivity and attracting goodness into my life.

indications for using Willow:

• For those who seem to be wet-blanket types.
• For those who feel that they are unrewarded by life.

keywords

Negative Victim mentality, bitterness, resentment, sulkiness, unfairness.
Positive Responsibility, humour, optimism, understanding.

Ulmus procera, Elm

Flowers in early spring. Pick catkins on twigs. Boiling method.

the Elm temperament

Elm types may become overwhelmed by a sense of over-responsibility. They are usually sensitive, strong and capable people and often work in a caring profession. However, exhaustion, due to extreme efforts to function with perfection, can sometimes lay them temporarily low. The Elm essence can bring forth the expression of confidence, the ability to cope and a strong sense of inner reliability.

affirmations

• I have all the strength I need to carry out my responsibilities.
• I can stay sensitive and responsible.
• I always find the strength to cope.
• Help is always there when I need it.

indications for using Elm

• For the carer who works, looks after the children and does the housework.
• For those who feel overwhelmed with the burden of work.
• For those who may become despondent at the responsibility of their task.
• For those who may have over-extended their commitments.

keywords

Negative Overwhelmed, inadequate, despondent, weak, over-extended, over-responsible.
Positive Able to delegate, realistic, confident, supported.

△ **Elm: Temporary feelings of inadequacy in responsible types.**

the over-care for the welfare of others group

Chicorium intybus, Chicory

Flowers in summer. Pick individual flowers. Sun potentized.

the Chicory temperament

Chicory types can appear loving, kind and generous but need to be appreciated. They are manipulative and self-pitying, and consider it the duty of loved ones to stay close by as they require constant attention. Critical of others, they find it difficult to let go and may use emotional blackmail to stay in control. The Chicory essence can bring forth genuine feelings of love and devotion, along with the ability to care for others without expecting or needing anything in return.

affirmations

- I nourish myself from within.
- As I let go I will find love and security lies within.
- Giving is all the reward I need.

indications for using Chicory

- For the pet, child or baby who demands attention all the time.
- For those who are over-possessive of their friends and family.
- For those who are critical of the smallest things.

△ **Chicory: a possessive and selfish attitude.**

> "Don't try to force anything, let life be a complete letting go. See God opening millions of flowers every day without forcing the buds."
>
> Bagwan Shree Rajneesh. *Dying for Enlightenment.*

keywords

Negative Over-protective, possessive, controlling, needy, self-pitying, manipulative.
Positive Unconditional love, letting go, giving, secure, respect.

Fagus sylvatica, Beech

Flowers in spring. Pick both male and female catkins on flowering twigs. Boiling method.

the Beech temperament

Beech types can be extremely inflexible and narrow-minded, as well as arrogant and hypercritical of others. They see only the negative side of a situation, sitting in judgement without any attempt to understand, as if the world itself intrudes upon their space. The Beech essence can bring forth tolerance and kindness, plus a greater understanding, so that they are better able to see the good in other people.

affirmations

- I am leaving myself and others alone.
- I have a right to be and others have a right to be.
- Everyone is growing in goodness.

indications for using Beech

- For those who cannot tolerate aspects of life that are completely outside

△ **Beech: for an intolerant and critical attitude to others.**

human control and cannot be changed, such as the weather.
- For those who are irritated by other people's trivial habits.
- For those who are critical of everyone and everything, but never offer a positive alternative.

keywords

Negative Intolerant, hypercritical, arrogant, isolated, judgemental.
Positive Tolerance, understanding, kindness, companionship.

△ **Vervain: over-effort or enthusiasm, thinking they are right.**

Verbena officinalis, Vervain

Flowers in summer. Pick tips of flowering spikes. Sun potentized.

the Vervain temperament

Vervain types have firm principles and think they are right. They are over-enthusiastic, intense and can get ahead of themselves. Often hyperactive, they suffer from stress or "nerves" and all manner of attendant physical ailments. They find it difficult to relax and, incensed by injustice, they can become fanatical. The Vervain essence can bring forth the ability to relax, let things be and allow others their opinions.

affirmations

- I can relax.
- I can let things take their course.
- I can let others be.

indications for using Vervain:

- For the child who is stressed or seems to be hyperactive.
- For executive types, that could be on the road to burnout.
- For those unable to stop and enjoy the fruits of their labour.
- For those who believe life should be an effort.

keywords

Negative Hyperactive, fanatical, over-enthusiastic, stressed, always right.
Positive Relaxation, accepting, objective, understanding, helpful.

Vitis vinifera, Vine

Flowers in late spring. Pick flowering sprigs. Sun potentized.

the Vine temperament

Vine types may be domineering, unscrupulous, ruthless and cruel, perhaps to disguise a weak inner core. The Vine essence is ideal for individuals who crave power, and for those who are controlling and bully others. It is also helpful when suffering from mental and physical inflexibility. This essence can bring forth inner strength, natural authority in teachers and leaders, and respect for others.

affirmations

- I am accepting the beauty in everyone's differences.
- It is a joy to help others help themselves.

indications for using Vine

- For the child who is a bully at school and on the street.
- For those who give orders and expect instant obedience.
- For those who order others about, even when ill.
- For those who dominate the weak.

keywords

Negative Domineering, ruthless, craving power, inflexible, aggressive.
Positive Understanding, wisdom, leadership, strength, authority.

△ **Vine: a dictatorial bully.**

△ **Rock Water: the need to be seen as perfect.**

Rock Water

This is the only essence of the Bach system that is not derived from a flower. Sun potentized. Fill a bowl with water from a spring known to have healing qualities, and leave in the sun for one to three hours.

the Rock Water temperament

Rock Water types practise self-denial and are very hard on themselves, suppressing basic human needs. They can be highly disciplined, often following extreme religious practices. They are apparently aiming to be saints and an example to all while still on the earth. The Rock Water essence can bring kindliness, particularly to themselves.

affirmations

- I am letting a soft kindness into my inner being.
- I no longer feel the need to be better than I am.
- I like to relax and enjoy being me.

indications for using Rock Water

- For those who are hard taskmasters.
- For those who are rigid, often with physical stiffness.
- For those who find it difficult to relax and enjoy themselves.

keywords

Negative Perfection, asceticism, denial, discipline, rigidity, obsession, martyrdom.
Positive Flexible, open-minded, relaxed, kind, fun-loving, emotional.

Using flower essences internally

Flower essences are usually taken internally using a small dropper bottle from which a number of drops are taken several times a day, depending on the brand of essence in use. These bottles are easy to use and a course of treatment can normally be fitted into the daily routine without forgetting. No special rules apply, as they do in other healing systems such as homeopathy, so you are free to eat and drink anything at any time and use your usual toothpaste.

It is advisable to take the drops morning and night, when the system is clear, and also before meals, holding them in the mouth for a few moments. A rhythmical approach like this, if you can adhere to it, will give the best results. No advantage is gained by taking a double dose if the previous dose has been forgotten, as taking more than the suggested number of drops is a waste.

△ **Still spring water and brandy form the liquid base in dosage bottles.**

Preparing a dosage bottle for Bach essences

You may find it helpful to make up more than one bottle – say, one to put by the bed and one to leave in the kitchen, or one to leave at work for the daytime doses and one at home for the evening and weekends. Small dropper bottles are available from pharmacies.

Almost fill a 30ml/1fl oz dropper bottle with spring water. Add 5ml/1 tsp brandy or vodka as a preservative. Use cider vinegar or glycerine if you wish to avoid alcohol. For babies and animals you can omit the preservative, in which case the bottle must be kept in the fridge.

△ **1** Add 2 drops of each of your chosen essences to the water and brandy in the bottle.

△ **2** Label the bottle with the name of the person being treated, the date and a list of the contents.

dosage instructions

Take 4 drops, four times a day for three weeks, then allow a week to integrate and assess what to put in a new bottle. Each treatment is based on a four-week cycle, in harmony with the cycle of the moon.

Essences for long-term treatment can be taken in a glass of water. Add 2 drops of each chosen essence to the glass and stir well to activate the essences. Sip four times a day, making a fresh batch daily. If you cannot tolerate alcohol, add the essence to a glass of hot water, as this will cause the alcohol to evaporate. Essences can also be taken directly from the stock bottle, by putting 2 to 4 drops under the tongue, although this approach is not thought to be as effective, as they are absorbed more efficiently when diluted.

△ **3** Mix the contents well by banging the bottle on the palm of the hand.

preparing flower essences in pill form

Impregnating sugar or lactose pills with flower essences can prove a very user-friendly way of ingesting them. Weigh 30g/1oz pilules and fill a small jar, add 2 drops of each chosen essence and shake well. Pour the pills on to a clean plate, spread out and allow to dry. Return them to the jar and chew two pills thoroughly as required, preferably with water.

how many essences?

Traditional Bach literature, written since the 1930s, recommends that no more than a total of six essences should be combined in a treatment bottle. Many flower blends on the market, as well as the Bach combinations presented in this book, contain more than ten essences. However, they are designed to work together on a single issue, which seems to be a critical factor. Treating a number of diverse issues with too many essences all at once, may dilute the effect, leaving nothing properly addressed. In practice, there is a certain amount of usable "psychic space" and, as the bands of colours in a rainbow lay side by side, so the chosen essences fill such a space with their differing healing vibrations.

Some essence producers suggest that one well-chosen essence that addresses a core issue can be very effective and also seems to eliminate many related issues, which at the original consultation seemed

△ **Two drops of an essence in a glass of water is an effective way of treating a passing mood.**

▷ **The quantity of water used is not important, the essences are effective at any strength.**

to demand treatment. A small study reported in Donna Cunningham's *Flower Remedies Handbook* (1992), tested the effects of taking either one, four or seven essences. The results suggested that four essences were actually more effective than one or seven, and a number of producers do suggest four. A general guideline in most cases would seem to be that a treatment bottle should contain no more than six, but preferably four, essences.

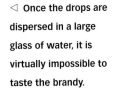

◁ **Once the drops are dispersed in a large glass of water, it is virtually impossible to taste the brandy.**

treatment period

It is difficult to say for how long essences will be required, as there is no way of knowing the depth of the issue being addressed or what other lessons could come up along the way, which will need to be cleared to effect a complete resolution. An acute problem, such as not sleeping, can sometimes be resolved with one treatment bottle, and some essence makers – though not all – are of the opinion that if you forget to take the drops, it is a sign that treatment is no longer required. For most difficulties, however, it is advisable to take three bottles, and some chronic problems could require in excess of four to facilitate long-lasting improvement.

essences and other therapies

Flower essences are very compatible with other therapies and many health practitioners use them in addition to a wide range of other modalities, including allopathic medicine. The reason essences do not interfere with other means of therapy is that they work on a higher level and may even enhance treatment, as they energize the human system. Negative thinking may often prove an obstacle to healing, so if a more positive frame of mind is encouraged, greater improvement may be enjoyed.

Using flower essences externally

The wide use of flower essences in oils and creams confirms their powerful effect topically and many therapists believe that such usage greatly enhances the effect of the flowers. Dr Bach himself was reported to have used flower essences externally and in some of his early case histories he recommended that any pain, stiffness or inflammation should be treated externally with compresses.

flower essence baths

Some makers suggest putting the flower essences in warm baths, taking four spaced throughout the day and relaxing in each one for twenty minutes. Four baths a day is not a practical option for some, but the addition of 12 drops of the current dosage mixture, or 4 drops of each chosen essence, to the clean bath water can be very supportive to treatment. Essential oils can also be added for greater enjoyment and healing. Swirl the water in a figure of eight to activate the essences and soak for twenty minutes. While relaxing, make a point of thinking positive thoughts, perhaps repeating the affirmations which relate to the chosen essences.

Preparing a flower essence cream

Apply flower essence cream to the affected area twice daily, or as required. A few drops of an essential oil can be added to the cream to enhance its healing properties.

ingredients
- Hypoallergenic, non-perfumed base cream
- Flower essences
- Essential oil (optional)

equipment
- Jar with lid
- Wooden stick or straw

1 Fill the jar with 50g/2oz cream. You can also use your favourite moisturizer as a base if you prefer, but avoid any strongly scented creams.
2 Add 4 drops of each chosen essence and 4 drops of essential oil, if liked. Limit the number of chosen essences to four, as too many drops can make the cream too liquid.
3 Mix with the wooden stick or a stiff straw, which should then be discarded.
4 Wipe the top of the jar before screwing on the cap.

▷ **Use a hypoallergenic cream with no perfume.**

Preparing a flower essence compress

A hot or cold compress can be useful for sprains, bruising, bites or burns. Lay it on the affected area and repeat until relief is felt, but seek medical advice if appropriate.

ingredients
- Hot or cold water
- Ice (optional)
- Chosen flower essences
- Lavender essential oil, particularly for burns

equipment
- Bowl
- Clean flannel or cotton wool

1 Fill the bowl with hot or cold water, adding ice to cool the water further if necessary.
2 Add 4 drops of each chosen flower essence and 4 drops essential oil to the water.
3 Soak the flannel or cotton wool in the water, wring out and place on the affected area.

▷ **Making a flower essence compress.**

◁ **After a flower essence bath take time to relax, wrapped in towels or in loose-fitting clothes, to fully absorb the beneficial effects.**

Preparing a flower essence spray

Sprays are a marvellous way of using essences, ideal for cleansing a home of negative energy or for cleansing the treatment room between clients. Adding essential oils brings not only added healing benefits, but also a wonderful uplifting smell. Lighter oils such as Lavender, Geranium or Lemon Grass work best. The heavier oils such as Ylang Ylang or Mandarin can clog the spray nozzle.

ingredients
• Spring water
• Chosen essential oil
• Chosen flower essences

equipment
• Plastic or glass spray bottle
• Measuring jug

◁ **Making your own spray mixtures gives a wide choice of mood enhancers.**

1 Fill the bottle with 50ml/2fl oz spring water.

2 Add a total of 10 drops of essential oil.

3 Add 4 drops of each chosen flower essence.

4 Shake the bottle to activate the essences and spray around the room twice daily, or as required.

△ **A flower essence spray can be used on yourself as well as in a room.**

Using flower essences with massage

Mixing essences in massage oil can greatly enhance the treatment.

ingredients
• Essential oil
• Chosen flower essences
• 50ml/2fl oz cold-pressed almond oil

1 Put 4 drops of essential oil and 4 drops of chosen flower essences into a bottle and add the almond oil.

2 Shake the bottle to mix, then pour into a small bowl and use immediately.

▷ **Applying an oil that contains flower essences before and after exercise may reduce stiffness and lessen the risk of any strained or aching muscles.**

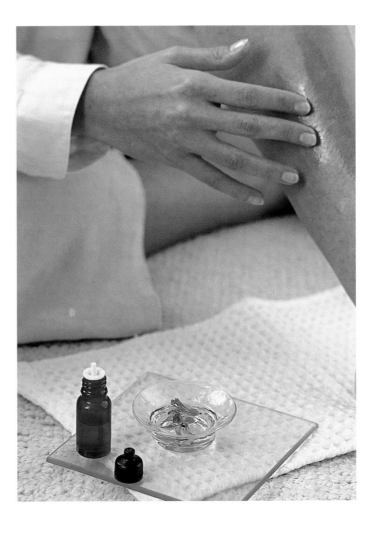

FLOWER ESSENCE MASSAGE MIXTURE

• Dandelion, to relax the muscles.

• Comfrey, to relax the musculature, skeleton and joints.

• Chamomile, to relax the involuntary muscles.

• Rock Water, an excellent addition that helps to relax rigidity in the whole of your system.

• Vervain, to release stress and tension.

• Orange Hawkweed, to release trauma and any energy blocks that have built up in the system.

Bach essences for emergencies

Five of the Bach essences are blended together to make a wonderful addition to a first-aid kit, the most famous version of which is known as Dr Bach's "Rescue Remedy". This emergency formula has proved to be extremely helpful in a broad range of stressful situations, for people, animals and plants, and is many people's first introduction to flower essence therapy. The five components of Rescue Remedy are:

Rock Rose	*terror and panic*
Impatiens	*irritability, tension and pain*
Cherry Plum	*fear of losing control, panic*
Clematis	*faintness, unconsciousness, faraway feelings*
Star of Bethlehem	*shock and panic*

Some equivalent composite remedies are known as Five Flower Formula, Emergency Essence, Recovery Remedy, Calming Essence and R.Q. Here, rather than referring to specific brands, Emergency Essence is used as a generic description. It can bring calm,

△ **rock rose**

△ **cherry plum**

△ **clematis**

△ **impatiens**

△ **star of Bethlehem**

and serenity, and quickly restore balance to the system. Keep some at home, at work, and in the car and always carry it with you

for emergencies. If you are new to essences, the Emergency Essence is ideal as an introduction. Use it before interviews, hospital appointments, visits to the doctor or dentist, operations and accidents, after major or minor arguments, when you are coping with difficult children, bad news, panic attacks, childbirth, stress at work, deadlines, performance nerves, or from grief and bereavement.

dosage instructions

- In case of emergencies, take 4 drops in a small glass of water and sip slowly until you are calm. If no liquid is available, take the drops directly on your tongue. Take every few minutes, as the effect is cumulative.
- When a difficult event is approaching, make up a dosage bottle. Add 4 drops of the Emergency Essence to a 30ml/1fl oz dropper bottle of spring water. Add 5ml/ 1 tsp brandy and shake well. Take doses four times a day. You can take up to ten doses the day before and one every ten minutes just before the event, if required.
- If things are stressful at home, put

▷ **If no liquid is available, take the drops directly on the tongue. More than one dose may be required.**

100ml/3½fl oz spring water in a plastic spray bottle, add 12 drops of the Emergency Essence and shake well. Add an essential oil such as Lavender for the calming effect and attractive perfume, and spray at will around the rooms twice a day.

- The Emergency Essence can be used as a single essence in a dosage bottle if you expect to be in an extreme situation for some time. Add 4 drops of the stock to the treatment bottle along with other chosen essences, if needed.

using the Emergency Essence in cream form

This combination has proved excellent in cream form and has had excellent results in the relief of stings, bites, bruises, cuts, allergic reactions, aches or pains, rashes, burns, blisters and skin complaints. A wide range of Emergency Creams are available for purchase but it is just as easy to prepare your own if you have some liquid stocks.

preparing your own cream

Add 10 drops of the Emergency Essence to 50g/2oz of a hypoallergenic base cream and mix. Alternatively, 3 drops of each of the five individual stocks can be used. Up to 4 drops of Lavender and/or Tea Tree essential oil are useful healing additions. The addition of 3 drops of Crab Apple stock is helpful, particularly if the cream is prepared for soothing a skin complaint. Stir with a spoon or wooden stick, which can then be thrown away.

instructions for using the cream

- Apply immediately if possible. Bruises may not appear. Stings may come up, but can go down quickly depending on how much tissue damage has occurred. Cuts will heal quickly, as will blisters.
- Apply the cream every couple of minutes, as the body rapidly absorbs the healing energy of the essence. Continue for up to 15 minutes. If some discomfort remains treat every 15 minutes thereafter.
- If possible give the Emergency Essence internally in a liquid or on the tongue to aid the recovery process – the emotions are equally shocked by an external impact.
- If the cream is not available, pat liquid stock on the injury, which will work just as effectively.

suggestions for using Emergency Essence

- Dose ahead of time if you are nervous about your driving test, as some excellent results have been reported, including one woman who passed after 14 attempts. In such cases add Honeysuckle stock to the mix for forgetfulness of past failures.
- If you should encounter a car accident or similar emergency situation and feel drawn to help with the Emergency Essence, do not under any circumstances give it internally without permission. The victim may require an anaesthetic or have other problems. Rubbed on pulse points such as wrists and forehead, it will prove equally effective.
- For burns, put 12 drops in a bowl of very cold water, add ice if necessary and either immerse the burnt area, or soak a clean cloth in the water and place on the burn. Resoak the cloth frequently to cool it.
- To cleanse a cut or graze, put 12 drops in a bowl of warm or cold water, as required, and soak some cotton wool. Gently cleanse the area, and leave the cotton wool on for a time to allow the healing energy to be absorbed. Remove and leave to dry. A little cream can be applied before covering with a plaster or bandage.

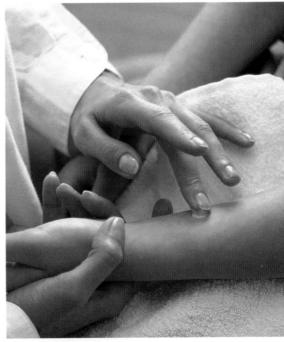

△ Apply cream every few minutes, wiping off excess, as the body rapidly absorbs the healing energy of the essence.

Bach flower essence combinations

One of the most difficult challenges when first starting to use flower essences is to know which ones to choose, but in formulating Rescue Remedy from five flower essences, Dr Bach himself paved the way for the use of combinations, or mixtures of essences designed for specific purposes.

More recently, observation of patterns of essences that are helpful in particular circumstances has led to the formulation of other combinations. The mixtures are not marketed as such, but are for you to make up at home, or to ask your friendly flower essence shop or practitioner to make up as an inexpensive treatment bottle. Interestingly, with the ever more widespread use of dowsing and kinesiology, some flower essence stockists are now permitting their clients to choose intuitively and make up their own personal combinations. Considering that some stockists now keep more than 500 different essences in stock form, this is a most helpful and proactive way of increasing access and helping people to help themselves. Very few of us could afford to buy a range of that size.

You might want to try some of the following combinations, suggested by Andrew Tresidder. If you have difficulty selecting one to start with, you might try a four to six week course of Relationship Mix, which has had great benefits for many people that have used it. Alternatively, many people carry unresolved sadness below the surface. Even if this is deeply buried, Change and Bereavement Mix or Blues Mix are superb combinations to help resolve such issues. Again, a course of several weeks will be of benefit.

△ **Heather**

▷ **Many people now have daily access to a complete set of Bach flower essences, either at home or in the workplace.**

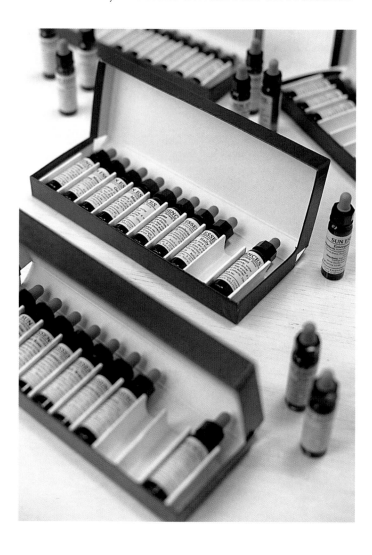

Relationship Mix

Chicory, Gentian, Heather, Holly, Impatiens, Mustard, Pine, Red Chestnut, Sweet Chestnut, Vine, Walnut and Willow.

For clear and honest communication and for forgiveness.

Anger Mix

Beech, Cherry Plum, Holly, Impatiens, Pine, Vine and Willow.

For anger and irritation, for any wish to dominate, for control, for jealousy, or for bitterness and resentment.

Confidence Mix

Centaury, Chestnut Bud, Gentian, Larch, Pine, Sweet Chestnut, Walnut and Wild Rose.

Builds inner confidence and constancy.

Study and Intuition Mix

Cerato, Chestnut Bud, Clematis, Impatiens, Rock Water, Scleranthus, White Chestnut and Wild Oat. On occasions Wild Rose may be added.

Helps concentrated study, with enthusiasm and without inner distractions.

Change and Bereavement Mix

Chestnut Bud, Gentian, Gorse, Heather, Honeysuckle, Mustard, Pine, Star of Bethlehem, Sweet Chestnut, Walnut, Wild Rose and Willow.

Valuable for all who have been bereaved, even in the distant past, this mix also helps you to cope with the changing circumstances of life.

△ **Mustard**

△ **White Chestnut**

△ **Wild Oat**

Carers and Worriers Mix

Agrimony, Gentian, Heather, Red Chestnut, White Chestnut. For sleeplessness you can also add Vervain.

Carers often carry a heavy burden for a long time, both emotionally and physically. Therefore, Exhaustion Mix is an ideal accompaniment to this mix to help refresh and regenerate.

Exhaustion Mix

Elm, Gorse, Hornbeam, Mustard, Oak, Olive, Walnut and Wild Rose.

Useful as a pick-me-up after prolonged effort; also for those with responsibilities that sometimes feel too heavy.

Leadership Mix

Beech, Centaury, Cerato, Chestnut Bud, Elm, Heather, Holly, Impatiens, Oak, Red Chestnut, Rock Water, Scleranthus, Star of Bethlehem, Vervain, Vine, Walnut and Wild Oat.

Helps leaders to stay in emotional balance.

Addictions Mix

Agrimony, Cherry Plum, Clematis, Crab Apple, Gentian, Larch, Pine, Rock Rose, Star of Bethlehem, Walnut and White Chestnut.

This mix helps break psychological dependencies by strengthening emotional reserves. One of the main reasons addictions develop is insecurity – while small children may overcome this by sucking their thumbs, adults often adopt

more harmful habits. This combination will usually need to be followed with a course of Relationship Mix.

Fears and Nightmares Mix

Aspen, Cherry Plum, Mimulus, Rock Rose, Star of Bethlehem and White Chestnut.

For fears, terrors and nightmares, in both adults and children.

Work Stress Mix

Gentian, Hornbeam, Impatiens, Mustard, Olive, Rock Water, Vervain, Walnut and White Chestnut.

Refreshes and restores interest when you are stressed at work. Emergency Essence is also useful in this situation.

△ **Pine**

Follow your Heart Mix

Centaury, Cerato, Chestnut Bud, Pine, Rock Water and Wild Oat.

To help you follow your intuition and the path in life that is best for you, even if it is not obvious at present. Also helps to gain wisdom from life's experiences.

Blues Mix

Gentian, Gorse, Mustard, Sweet Chestnut, Walnut, Wild Rose and Willow.

Helps lift low moods and sadness, and allows the sunshine back into life. Do not use it instead of prescribed conventional antidepressants, and always seek medical advice for feelings of depression.

Past Abuse Mix

Agrimony, Crab Apple, Gentian, Gorse, Holly, Mustard, Pine, Rock Rose, Star of Bethlehem, Sweet Chestnut, Walnut and Willow.

For cases of past emotional and physical abuse. Most adults carry the scars of past hurts at a feeling level, however well the effects have been dealt with in later life.

Insomnia Mix

Impatiens, Rock Rose, Vervain and White Chestnut.

Useful for releasing mental and emotional patterns and for soothing and quietening any mental excitement that prevents refreshing sleep.

The following recently discovered essences, a number of which were initially prepared and researched by the Flower Essence Society in California, complement and extend the range of choice. Providing some very specific and useful healing properties, they have proved to be of great service to consumers and practitioners. They are highly effective in their treatment of people and animals, and consistent and positive results are frequently reported.

These essences are made from a selection of common wild flowers; it is exciting to understand that there is far more to the familiar Dandelion than meets the eye. The new essences mix well with the Bach essences and are equally effective in combination with each other, or given as a single essence. The following groups of essences will make a valuable and hard-working addition to your collection.

essences for developing personal power and direction

Everyone suffers from low self-esteem at some time and it is thought to be the most common negative condition. With this affliction, the mind holds no vision of success so it is difficult for you to put yourself forward in life, this then deprives you of the chance to grow and learn. The following golden essences can build strength, confidence and self-love. Particularly helpful for setting personal boundaries, they can assist the discovery of your true potential, helping to harness your talents and enabling you to find direction and live life to the full.

Helianthus annuus, Sunflower

When the male aspects of the personality are underdeveloped, they can express themselves in extreme ways. Sunflower essence can balance such underdeveloped or overdeveloped egos and bring greater empowerment. It becomes possible to radiate outwards, like the flower does, and reach for the sun, or for the peaks of personal achievement.

indications for using Sunflower

- For those of either sex who have difficulties expressing their male qualities in a balanced fashion.
- For those who have conflict with authority figures.
- For those who are suffering from an ongoing damaged relationship with the dominant parent.

keywords

Negative Bombastic, egotism, boastfulness, self-effacement and aggrandisement.
Positive Warm, radiant, positive, action, compassion, individuality, belief, assertiveness.

Ranunculus bulbosus, Buttercup

This essence is indicated when there is a lack of self-esteem. Buttercup warms and nourishes the being with golden light. It brings an understanding of how special and unique life is, no matter how humble your lot may seem.

△ **Sunflower: empowerment of the male qualities.**

△ **Buttercup: recognizing your uniqueness.**

indications for using Buttercup

- For those who compare themselves to others and appear wanting.
- For those who do not feel worthy.
- For those who feel that their contribution to life has no value.
- For those who have a disability, particularly children.

keywords

Negative Worthlessness, envy, valueless, doubt, belittling.
Positive Recognition, joy, abundance, value, contribution, unique, special.

Solidago virgaurea, Goldenrod

Goldenrod essence strengthens self-respect and a sense of self, giving encouragement to stand up for what you know underneath is right and to value your own knowledge, feelings and intuition. The Goldenrod essence helps you to live life in response to your own integrity instead of in reaction or submission to other influences.

indications for using Goldenrod

- For those who feel diminished, crushed or swayed – by authority figures, bullying, social pressures or outside influences.
- For those who deny their own understanding and integrity.
- For those who did not receive adequate fathering in childhood and are still feeling the lack of it.
- For those who are stuck in resentment or childish rebelliousness, instead of asserting themselves.

keywords

Negative Powerlessness, inferiority, submission, resentment, rebelliousness.
Positive Integrity, self-respect, authoritativeness, assertiveness.

△ **Goldenrod: strengthens inner authority and self-respect.**

△ **Tansy: purposeful drive and direction.**

Tanacetum vulgare, Tansy

When there is a lack of motivation, procrastination and a poor sense of self, it becomes difficult to see a way forward. Tansy essence can help you find a solid centre within yourself, which will bring an instinctive sense of the right direction and propel you forward into action.

indications for using Tansy

- For those who are capable and talented, but hold back.
- For those who seem aloof and nonchalant and avoid involvement with life.

keywords

Negative Lethargy, suppression, lazy, stagnant, procrastination, sluggishness, delay.
Positive Decisive, purposeful, action, direction, expression.

Verbascum thapsus, Mullein

Mullein is the remedy to bring inner light and is indicated when it seems difficult to be true to your conscience. There may be an element of dishonesty in daily interactions, which may be partly unconscious due to denial or conditioning. This essence can bring the courage and strength to be true to yourself and embrace your rightful path in life. Mullein can be supportive for exploring a sense of individuality in the face of possible opposition.

△ **Mullein: inner truthfulness and conscience.**

indications for using Mullein:

- For those who feel unable to stand by their beliefs.
- For those who go against themselves to please others.
- For those who need help to face the truth in a situation.
- For those who feel weak and confused, and are unable to hear their inner voice.

keywords

Negative Doubt, denial, dishonesty, deceit, conditioning.
Positive Conviction, high morals, guidance, inner listening, discrimination, awareness, personal truth.

FURTHER SUGGESTIONS

- Combine Tansy, Buttercup, Mullein, Golden Rod and Sunflower for a supportive blend for confidence and new direction.
- Add Larch for an additional confidence booster.
- Add Wild Rose if there is apathy or resignation about life.
- Add Walnut to give protection from outside influences while moving forward in a new direction.
- Wild Oat is helpful in finding your true life path.

essences for mental work

You have a report to write, memos to read, a letter to finish: so it goes, on and on. This selection of flower essences can help support the thinking process while you are forming new ideas. The following essences can clear the head, improve concentration, keep the mind clear, refreshed and balanced and give that little boost to get you across the finishing line.

Put the essences into a glass or bottle of water and sip as required while you are working.

△ **Shasta Daisy: encourages a holistic viewpoint.**

Leucanthemum x *superbum,* Shasta Daisy

Shasta Daisy essence is helpful for those who are scattered thinkers or have the tendency to focus on parts. This essence is designed to pull all the various pieces into a unified whole, making it possible to enjoy a more complete overview.

indications for using Shasta Daisy
• For those who are thinking out a project and wish to see it as a more unified whole.
• For therapists who would like to gain a more holistic view of their client's situation.

keywords
Negative Over-intellectualism, scattered, over-analytical.
Positive Synthesis, meaning, integration, insight, perspective, wholeness.

Mentha x *piperita,* Peppermint

Peppermint essence can help to clarify and cool down the thinking processes at times of great emotional strain or extreme mental activity, clearing a clouded mind.

△ **Peppermint: clearing the thinking processes.**

indications for using Peppermint
• For those who feel sluggish after eating.
• For those who need stimulants to feel more awake.

keywords
Negative Apathetic, sluggish, dull, craving food, unbalanced.
Positive Energy, alertness, mental clarity, concentration, lightness, cooling.

Rubus fruticosus, Blackberry

This essence is indicated when a person has lots of ideas but seems unable to find enough will to bring them into reality, perhaps due to the perceived pain of living. Blackberry can harness power and energy and help you to focus on and attain your goal without distraction.

indications for using Blackberry
• For those who have grand thoughts but seem to accomplish little.
• For those who need to set goals, but lack the ability to get organized.

△ **Blackberry: grounds ideas in reality.**

keywords
Negative Confusion, denial, living in ideas, immobility, inertia.
Positive Action, insight, creation, manifestation, motivation, construction, focus, will.

Tropaeolum majus, Nasturtium

This essence is helpful for the dry, intellectual types who tend to drift into the realms of thought and detach from feelings, which may weaken the physical body. Nasturtium can also help to revitalize the mind after periods of intensive study.

indications for using Nasturtium
• For those who need balance after intense worry or mental activity.
• For those who are over-intellectual and lack physical vitality.

keywords
Negative Obsessive, intense, drained, intellectualism, weakness.
Positive Balance, vitality, radiance, health.

△ **Nasturtium: balancing energy.**

FURTHER SUGGESTIONS
• These essences work particularly well with Hornbeam, and also Olive and Oak if projects become very pressured.
• Chestnut Bud makes it easier to learn.
• Beech and Tansy can prove useful additions.
• Gentian is helpful if there are setbacks – for instance, if a piece of work is not acceptable and needs to be rewritten.

essences for living lightly and with humour

Taking these essences can bring a lighter, more open and objective viewpoint, releasing the need to be focused on yourself and your personal problems. This new optimistic frame of mind helps life to seem lighter, more abundant, enjoyable, bright and promising.

△ **Borage: lightness of heart.**

Borago officinalis, Borage

Use Borage essence when there is great heaviness and sadness in the heart. It can break through the dark to reveal an inner lightness, which brings support, optimism and renewed courage.

indications for using Borage

• For those who feel broken-hearted.
• For those who need to feel more lightness in life.
• For those who need to rise above their difficulties.

keywords

Negative Grief, discouragement, heavy heart, constrictions.
Positive Cheerfulness, courage, buoyancy, uplifting.

Narcissus pseudonarcissus, Daffodil

Daffodil essence is indicated when your talents seem insignificant to you. This essence can bring recognition of their obvious worth and facilitate greater self-understanding and appreciation. A more individualistic path can be followed with a positive attitude. Life can blossom and the heart open to a new abundance.

△ **Daffodil: appreciation of your talents.**

indications for using Daffodil

• Supportive when deciding upon a career, particularly if it is an unusual one.
• For those who need to appreciate themselves more.
• For those who seek more abundance in their lives.

keywords

Negative Depression, self-doubt, worthlessness, constriction.
Positive Cleansing, uplifting, joy, happiness, abundance, appreciation, alignment.

Primula vulgaris, Primrose

Primrose is indicated when difficulties from childhood affect your life, perhaps through melancholia and deep unexplained sadness. Crushed and repressed feelings are gently released as this essence nourishes and comforts the inner child. The Primrose essence helps you start anew, pure and unblemished, with a lighter approach to life.

△ **Primrose: gives comfort and lightness for the inner child.**

indications for using Primrose

• Helpful for those doing inner-child work.
• For anyone who feels sad or low.

keywords

Negative Sadness, melancholia, depression, trauma, crushing, repression.
Positive Lightness, soft, refreshed, cleansed, nurturing, comfort.

Zinnia elegans, Zinnia

When there is over-seriousness and a lack of humour, Zinnia essence brings playful joy and a more detached view of the self.

indications for using Zinnia

• For those who take life too seriously and are unable to see the funny side.
• For those who cannot laugh at themselves.

keywords

Negative Dull, serious, dutiful, repressed.
Positive Exuberance, involvement, humour, lightness, spontaneity, playfulness, festivity.

△ **Zinnia: joyfulness and humour restored.**

FURTHER SUGGESTIONS

• Combine Borage, Daffodil, Primrose and Zinnia to give a combination for lightening the spirit.
• Add Elm to help you get through a stressful and busy time like Christmas with good humour and enjoyment.
• The addition of Gentian, Mustard or Gorse can be helpful, depending on the problem.

essences for strengthening the constitution

These essences are selected to support and boost the immune system. They are useful as a course to take at the beginning of winter if you have a tendency to succumb to infections such as colds, coughs, flu or other viruses at this time of year. They are also used for when you have difficulty making a full recovery as they help to speed up the process.

△ **Jack-by-the-hedge: helps to support a delicate immune system.**

Alliaria petiolata, Jack-by-the-hedge

Jack-by-the-hedge is ideal for the emotional type who may have a delicate constitution and is prone to infection or allergic reactions. This essence can help support the heart connection to the body's defence system, making it an ideal choice when emotional pain, such as grief, has weakened the constitution.

indications for using Jack-by-the-hedge
• For those who often feel out of sorts or under the weather.
• For those who suffer from allergies.

keywords
Negative Low, fragile, sensitive, weak, sickly.
Positive Well, supportive, strength, resilience.

Allium ursinum, Ramsons

This essence can help to bring white light into the body, to cleanse a sluggish, toxic system which, if not corrected, could debilitate and deplete the immune system. The Ramsons essence can raise vitality

△ **Ramsons: supports the body's defences against toxic influences.**

levels and resistance to infection. It is excellent as a spring cleanser, but also as a boost to the body's defences at the beginning of winter.

indications for using Ramsons
• For those who are lethargic and run down.
• For those who find it difficult to shake off illness.
• For those who suffer from chronic, toxic conditions.

keywords
Negative Toxic, congested, sluggish.
Positive Radiance, invigorated, enlivening, renewing, cleansing.

Prunella vulgaris, Self-heal

Self-heal can be used in all healing situations. It re-energizes the healing life-force from within, reducing the need to seek support from others. Self-heal essence brings forth responsibility for healing the self through very difficult life challenges.

△ **Self-heal: to access the healer within.**

indications for using Self-heal
• For those who need to engage more energetically with life.
• For those who believe they cannot help themselves.

keywords
Negative Irresponsibility, dependency.
Positive Vitality, recuperation, rejuvenation, self-trust.

Viola tricolor, Pansy

Pansy has a predominantly physical application, helping to strengthen the body's defence mechanisms against viral attack and lifting energy levels. It is excellent in creams for infectious skin conditions.

indications for using Pansy
• For those who are susceptible to frequent colds or non-specific infections.
• For those who need to improve their energy levels after a long illness.

keywords
Negative Infection, viruses, weakness, susceptibility to colds.
Positive Strength, resistance, hardiness.

△ **Pansy: Resists viral infection.**

FURTHER SUGGESTIONS
• Add Crab Apple for cleansing.
• Add Olive and Oak for further strengthening.
• Add the type remedy for mental, emotional and physical balance.
• Should there be a setback during recovery, add Gentian.

essences for relaxation and good sleep

The following essences are wonderful for those with demanding lifestyles, as they relax the body, enabling you to function in a more calm, focused and productive way. They are also helpful for restless sleepers.

△ **Chamomile: an excellent essence for children.**

Anthemis cotula, Chamomile

Chamomile is useful when there is emotional turmoil, which creates stress, sleeplessness and digestive problems.

indications for using Chamomile
• For emotionally based stomach problems, particularly in children.
• For babies who may be teething.

keywords
Negative Moodiness, hyperactivity, fussiness, colic, fretfulness, insomnia.
Positive Calming, stabilizing, soothing, sunny, balanced.

Hyacinthoides non-scripta, Bluebell (mixed colours)

The fresh, uplifting quality of a bluebell, and the peacefulness of the wood is embodied in this healing essence. Useful in times of extreme emotional difficulties.

indications for using Bluebell
• For those who are extremely distressed.
• For trauma and stress in animals.
• For those who are depressed.

keywords
Negative Overwrought, uptight, depressed, trauma, loss of self, stress.
Positive Peaceful, happy, uplifted, contentment, joy, confidence, tranquillity.

△ **Bluebell: nature's emergency essence.**

Hypericum perforatum, St John's Wort

St John's Wort flower essence is helpful for over-sensitive and vulnerable individuals, who may suffer from allergies or fears and are susceptible to stress. This essence strengthens the aura and promotes trust. Very helpful for children, it eases night fears and brings a sense of security.

indications for using St John's Wort
• For those who suffer from seasonal depression.
• For those who are frightened of the dark.
• For those who are sensitive to light.

keywords
Negative Fear, vulnerability, seasonal depression, nightmares, disturbed, over-sensitive.
Positive Strength, light, ease, rootedness.

Ipomoea purpurea, Morning Glory

This essence can be useful when leading an erratic lifestyle, often requiring stimulants to stay alert. Morning Glory essence gently regulates the body clock.

△ **St John's Wort: for children with night fears.**

△ **Morning Glory: a balancing essence.**

indications for using Morning Glory
• For those who rely on stimulants to help them through the day.
• For those who find it difficult to wake up in the morning.
• For those suffering from nervous tension.

keywords
Negative Addictions, fatigue, erratic, dull, hyperactive, depletion.
Positive Balance, awake, energy.

Taraxacum officinale, Dandelion

Dandelion is helpful for an over-stressed lifestyle. This essence can help you to relax and cope with everyday life.

indications for using Dandelion
• For those who have muscle tension.
• For those who have too much going on in their lives.

keywords
Negative Tension, striving, driving, intensity, perfectionism, unexpressed emotion.
Positive Effortless energy, inner ease, balance, wellbeing, relaxation.

△ **Dandelion: an ideal remedy for tension.**

essences to give protection

Sensitive individuals may become drained by the constant and unnatural demands of the modern environment, with its noise, pollution, smells, crowds, computers and the stressful emotions of other people in crowded places such as the underground. Flower essences in a spray, administered around the aura morning and night, or in the consulting room before and after a client's visit, can prove of enormous benefit. The addition of essential oil, such as Lavender, is very pleasant and, along with the aura cleansing technique described opposite, provides essential self-care.

Achillea millefolium, Pink Yarrow

Pink Yarrow is for those who are over-empathic and may absorb the negative feelings of others. This can cause emotional confusion as they may have difficulty differentiating their feelings from those of others, and thus feel drained. This essence can strengthen and protect the aura, which is also of great value to therapists working with clients.

indications for using Pink Yarrow

- For animals who are affected by their owner's emotions.
- For those who over-identify with others.

△ **Pink Yarrow: for protection from other people's emotions.**

△ **White Yarrow: helpful for increasing environmental protection.**

- For those who are particularly sensitive to disharmony.
- For therapists and healers to help them in working with clients.

keywords

Negative Absorbing, congestion, enmeshed, drained, merging, porous.
Positive Boundaries, protection, safety, self-contained, objective.

Achillea millefolium, White Yarrow

White Yarrow can help to protect the aura from negative environmental influences such as noise, fluorescent lights, industrial or traffic fumes or the positive ions emitted by office machinery and computers. This type may be sensitive to negative atmospheres in a house, thus feeling a debilitating energy drain. Yarrow can also give much needed protection to healers or individuals pursuing a spiritual path. The essence provides a shield of light, which gives essential protection from the energy-depleting activities. When it is prepared with sea water, White Yarrow is reported to be helpful for cleansing radiation.

indications for using White Yarrow

- For those who are overly sensitive to the frenetic pace of city life.
- For sensitive children who require extra protection.
- For those depleted by their environment.
- For those who suffer from allergies.

keywords

Negative Sensitive, drained, depletion, pollution, psychic toxicity, allergies, negativity.
Positive Shielded, invulnerable, protected, safe, boundaries, containment.

Mentha pulegium, Pennyroyal

Pennyroyal types may unconsciously absorb the negative thought-forms of others. They can suffer from psychic contamination or possession if their auric field is particularly weak. Pennyroyal gives protection from psychic attack and cleanses the thought processes, bringing clarity and independent action.

indications for using Pennyroyal

- For those who may be controlled by others.
- For those who suffer from mental confusion and obsession.
- For those who suffer from addiction.

△ **Pennyroyal: dissolves negative thought-forms.**

keywords

Negative Contamination, negativity, psychic possession, attack, addiction, obsessions, congestion.
Positive Purification, strengthening, clarity, positivity, integrity, vitality.

Pilosella aurantiaca, Orange Hawkweed

Orange Hawkweed essence is ideal in this group of essences for protection, as it can quickly transform anything that is not of the self into a purer and higher energy, thus preventing the settling-in of negativity. Also helpful in the treatment of shock, Orange Hawkweed can rebalance the system and clear repressed and blocked emotions, allowing deeper access to the true self. This essence can move the individual on to greater self-realization, expansion of consciousness and energy.

indications for using Orange Hawkweed

- A panacea essence for animals.
- Take for protection and before meditation for a deeper understanding of the self.
- Should an old injury be troublesome, a compress of this essence can prove helpful.
- For those feeling stuck, straightens things out, so all is as it should be.

△ **Orange Hawkweed: transforms anything that is not of the self.**

keywords

Negative Psychic attack, repression, confusion, trauma, stuck, blocked, negativity, shock.
Positive Grounding, flexible, objective, realization, transformation, expansion, energy.

61

FURTHER SUGGESTIONS

- The addition of Walnut, Centaury and Aspen can be of benefit.
- Combine all the essences into a spray and use as required.

△ **Centaury**

DOSAGE TIPS

- Essences can be taken internally if desired: take 7 drops 3 times a day.
- These essences can be added to a bath, in addition to whatever else is being taken in a treatment bottle.
- Add to oil burner and allow essences to permeate the house.

CLEANING THE AURA FOR PROTECTION

The effects of a flower essence spray are enhanced if the aura is "brushed clean" before application.

Cover the forehead with the fingertips overlapping and brush or stroke down the side of the face, neck and over the shoulder. Repeat this seven times. Then cover the crown with both fingertips and brush straight down the back to the coccyx: again, do this seven times. It is easier for a friend to do this for you, and you for them. However, if you are alone, it is possible to do it for yourself by splitting the back stroke into two, using the backs of the hands for the second half. Finally, spray the blend of essences up the front, over the head and down the back, then up one side, over the head and down the other side. Apply in the morning and then as required.

◁ **Many individuals prefer a topical approach to treatment and prepare their choice of essences in a spray. Mist your aura four times daily.**

Using flower essences in the home

In our modern lives we can suffer from stress and its effects more than anything else. Flower essences are a storehouse of natural healing, so try these easy ways to enable everyone to share in their benefits.

- Spray essences around the home; if chosen correctly, they can change the mood. Add essential oils and enjoy the lovely aromas.
- When washing clothes and bed linen, put some flower essence in the final rinse or add to a capful of fabric softener.

△ **Add flower essences to an oil burner so that everyone in the house can benefit from the healing energies.**

△ **Add a few drops of a favourite essence to a bowl of hand washing.**

▷ **To create a relaxing atmosphere, spray some essences around the bedroom before retiring, not forgetting to spray the bed. Try Red Rose essence to enhance passion.**

△ **Flower essence bathing products.**

- It can be difficult to remember to give essences to children – particularly during busy holiday periods, so put 4 drops of each chosen stock into a bottle of fruit squash, a carton of fruit juice or milk.
- If you are moving into a new home, add a combination of protection essences to the cleaning water to clear any residual energies from the previous owners. You could even consider adding them to the paint if you need to redecorate.
- Most people enjoy burning oils in an oil burner. When doing so, try adding some flower essences to the essential oil, so everyone will receive the benefits as the scents and healing energies permeate the house.
- Essences are great in the bath. Add them to the bath oil or the children's bubble bath.
- Adding essences to the wax during candle-making has been shown to work extremely well.
- Add flower essences to your face creams

or body lotions, as this will greatly support your regular cleansing and moisturizing beauty routines.

- Crab Apple essence with Pine essence and Pansy essence in a cream base is said to be excellent for skin complaints.
- Add essences to sun cream. The Australian Mulla Mulla essence is a specific for this. Otherwise, add Emergency Essence. It will help guard the family against the effects of sunburn.

general dosage instructions

- Add 2 drops of each essence stock to small quantities: about 30ml/1fl oz liquid, oil, or lotion, or 25g/1oz cream.
- Add 4 drops of each chosen stock to larger quantities: 50ml/2fl oz, 50g/2oz or more.
- If you are using essence from a dosage bottle formula, a minimum of 12 drops is recommended.
- Note: It is not necessary for the dilution to be exact for the essences to be effective.

Using Bach essences with astrology

Flower Essences can work well in harmony with other modalities such as Astrology. This partnership can prove particularly helpful if you are finding it difficult to clarify which of the twelve healers is your type essence. The twelve signs of the zodiac can be matched to the twelve healers and many find it of great interest to see which remedy belongs to your birth sign. For example, if you are born under the birth sign of Libra you are probably an indecisive individual. The healer essence Scleranthus is matched to this birth sign and being for indecision also, it is obviously a good choice.

Dr Bach in *The Twelve Healers* (1933), makes reference to astrology as a useful guide to choosing a helpful type essence for support along life's path. He suggests the moon's placement in the birth chart as providing the most valuable insight into a person's main lesson in life, and also their personality type, life's work and objectives. For example, if your moon were found in Scorpio, your matching type essence would be Chicory. The birth sign's matching essence will always be of great benefit in times of stress. However, the placement of other aspects of the birth chart such as the ascendant, and your birth sign's ruling planet are also helpful indicators in selecting further supportive type essences.

If you are interested in exploring this aspect of astrology further, a fully explained birth chart drawn up by an experienced astrologer will be of enormous value.

◁ **The twelve signs of the zodiac.**

THE TWELVE HEALERS AND THEIR CORRESPONDING ZODIAC SIGNS

Essence	Sign
Chicory	Scorpio
Mimulus	Capricorn
Agrimony	Sagittarius
Scleranthus	Libra
Clematis	Cancer
Centaury	Virgo
Gentian	Gemini
Vervain	Leo
Cerato	Taurus
Impatiens	Aries
Rock Rose	Pisces
Water Violet	Aquarius

Making Flower Essences

"And may we ever have joy and gratitude in our hearts that the Great Creator of all things, in his Love for us, has placed the herbs in the fields for our healing."

Dr E Bach. The Twelve Healers and Other Remedies 1933

Understanding nature

Nature's role in healing is not just a distillation of its products but also the power of its presence, which has an innate intelligence that can be contacted if approached in the right way. This begins with a simple love and respect for nature and above all, gratitude, which ought to be a natural thing because without food and oxygen it would not be possible to live. Unfortunately, many have become so divorced from nature that they have ceased to appreciate it.

From the essential foundation of gratitude comes a natural opening out to nature. Notice how your mind is behaving during a quiet walk in the woods; where is it actually focused? Probably towards yourself, and the endless thoughts that go round and round your head. Still the mind and let the consciousness go outward, look at everything, enjoy the light and air, and appreciate the beauty of nature, whatever the season. No matter how tired and stressed your system has become, nature's restorative powers can relax and calm, provided your heart and mind are receptive. Go for a walk in your bare feet, lean against a tree and look up through the leaves, lie down on the grass. These activities will allow nature's power to be absorbed more fully, and a sense of joy and oneness will be embraced and retained.

△ *"If you are seeking creative ideas go out walking. Angels whisper to a man when he goes for a walk."* Raymond Inman in *A Bag of Jewels*.

◁ The Easter Lily is a symbol of inner purity and helps us to reconcile tension between our spirituality and sexuality.

Focusing in minute detail on the structure of plants can enhance this experience of joy; the closer you look and the more appreciative attention you pay to nature, the more it is able to use this link to give back its healing energies. Many essence makers state that it is possible to hear the plants speak, but whatever your experience may be, just enjoy attuning with the energy of nature and allow it to improve your sense of wellbeing.

This continuing development of a strong connection with nature makes it easier to understand the healing gift of flower essences and is supportive to their preparation. Many producers now believe the energetic presence of the essence maker, thought of as the fifth element or spirit, is as essential to the process as the flowers themselves, in addition to the four

To Nature we look confidently for all the needs to keep us alive – air, light, food, drink and so on: it is not likely that in this great scheme which provides all, the healing of our illnesses and distress should be forgotten.

Edward Bach, *Wallingford lecture* (1936)

△ **Some believe the intelligence of nature can manifest as beings of light called Devas, which is Sanskrit for "shining ones". These entities are thought to oversee the growth of plants.**

◁ **"Nature patiently waits and we only have to turn back to her to find relief from our suffering." Dr Bach (1934).**

elements of nature. The essence maker is co-creating with nature, which is an exciting prospect. It is important to remember and reflect that the quality of an essence is not only dependent on the number of flowers, the location, fresh water and so on, but also on the respectful and reverent state of mind of the maker.

protecting nature

Out of a need to preserve and respect nature, most countries have policies restricting the picking of wild flowers, certainly of the rarer species. It is therefore advisable to check, perhaps at a local library, what rules apply before gathering flowers to make an essence. Essence makers also consider it respectful to seek permission to pick from the owner of the chosen site, and may go to considerable effort to get it. This provides additional protection, as it is not usually illegal to pick most common wild flowers on private land. Only a very small number of flowers are picked to make an essence, and this does not damage the plant. In many cases it will stimulate the plant to create more flowers, and therefore more seeds, which is ultimately beneficial.

Dr Bach hoped every home would have access to his essences and left preparation instructions so that everybody could make their own. Even if the investment of time to make the whole set is out of the question, just making a single essence is recommended as a unique opportunity to be part of a connection with nature and with the self-healing experience. All the tinctures made from the sun potentization and boiling methods have been reported in the Bach literature to be safe and non-toxic.

FOR A SUN-POTENTIZED ESSENCE

ingredients

- Three hours of clear, unclouded sunshine
- Fresh water
- Freshly opened flowers
- Brandy

equipment

- Thin glass bowl
- Scissors (optional)
- Unbleached filter papers
- Glass measuring jug
- Storage bottle
- Label(s)
- Pen

△ **Equipment for sun potentizing. You will also need a suitable basket for carrying the equipment to minimize possible breakages.**

▽ **Equipment for boiling. Purchase the essential items well in advance, and be ready for favourable weather.**

FOR BOILING A FLOWER ESSENCE

You need to set out on a dry day that will have sunny periods.

ingredients

- Fresh water
- Freshly flowering twigs
- Brandy

equipment

- Glass saucepan with lid
- Long-handled secateurs (pruning shears)
- Hooked walking stick
- Camping stove (if needed)
- Glass measuring jug
- Unbleached filter papers
- Storage bottles
- Label(s)
- Pen

glass bowls

It is important to find suitable thin glass bowls. Ideally, they must not have a pattern or ridging and should be very thin. The glass must be perfect with an ideal bowl shape, being small at the base and becoming larger at the top. Various, good, serviceable glass bowls can be found, but crystal finger bowls are found to make good essences. Unfortunately, they can be expensive.

picking the flowers

Nursing scissors have proved a good choice for essence making, being small with sharp points. If the idea of cutting the flowers

the morning before making the essence, but depending on the distance involved it may be necessary to visit the spring the previous evening. Store the water in clean glass bottles and keep it as cool as possible, leaving it outside over night, perhaps under a bush. Although this option is not ideal, it will still produce a very high-quality essence.

brandy

The brandy in the mother tinctures is used as a preservative only and an alcohol content of at least 16% is needed for the essence to remain stable. Any brand will do and although a 36% alcohol content, which is cheaper, may seem adequate, 40% is advised. Some of the boiled essences, despite filtering, may contain vegetable matter and many prepared by the sun potentization method will contain pollen. Should this organic content be unusually high for some reason, a fermentation process could occur which would spoil the essence. The use of the 40% proof brandy will give the mother tinctures a slightly higher alcohol content, ensuring that all the essences prepared will remain stable indefinitely.

sunshine

A clear, sunny day is vital to making a traditional flower essence. If clouds cover the sky half way through preparation it is advisable to give the essence back to the earth or drink it, returning on the next sunny day.

with scissors feels wrong, consider whether to pick the flowers by hand, as many essence producers do. Alternatively make a lasso from a stalk and gently pull the flowers off.

tips on the boiling method

Glass pans are ideal as they are easily cleaned. If the location is a long way from home, think about boiling the mother tincture out in the field. However, some camping stoves can take a long time to bring the pan to the boil, and you must be certain that there is enough gas. Filtering a bottled mother tincture takes patience, as many may be thick with sap and vegetable matter. Notice how the range of sensations can vary, from the heavenly almond smell of the Cherry Plum mother tincture to the vile taste of Walnut mother tincture.

water

Of great importance when making a flower essence, water is the medium on which the flowers are floated and in which their

energy is held. The ideal is fresh pure water from a spring near the flower's location, drawn just before making the essence. In some areas, this is possible, but in others it becomes more of a challenge if there is heavy agriculture and pollution. Some makers will suggest using a good quality bottled water but as this has been in the bottle an indefinite time, it may be "dead" and produce an inferior quality essence. It is worth researching the surrounding area in advance and locating a clean spring. Water can be collected early in

Making a flower essence

Through the process of making a flower essence Nature is able to reveal her healing powers. In this partnership with humanity her gifts can be bestowed.

a few days before

It is advisable to make only one essence at a time, so while visiting a particular location, sense which plant is "calling". Once this choice is made, walk around the community of flowers to get to know its size and the whereabouts of the various clumps. Spend some time in meditation beside the flowers. Drawing or photographing them can also help develop the close connection necessary for a high quality essence. Research into the flower's history and growth pattern can be very interesting, as well as giving insight into its character according to the doctrine of signatures.

the day before

Before the day on which you prepare a flower essence, clarify simple things like the best place to park for over four hours. Ensure that the car has enough fuel, and take suitable drinks, food and a rug to sit on. Pack a pad, pen or voice recorder to note down any thoughts you may have about the flowers, plus a camera or art materials to record the flowers, if you wish. Collect water the night before, if necessary, and make sure all essential equipment is sterilized and packed, including extra water to wash your hands.

Go to bed early, since if you are tired the next day the quality of the essence will suffer. An interesting study was done on this point during an expedition to make Rock Rose mother tincture. After an early start and a very long trip, the driver felt particularly tired and unwell. It was decided to make separate bowls and dowse the potency of each once the tinctures were "cooked". Although all three makers approached the procedure in exactly the same way, the potency of the driver's bowl was found to be significantly lower.

> The whole principle of Healing by this method is so simple it can be understood by almost everyone, and even the very Herbs themselves can be gathered and prepared by any who take delight in such.
>
> Edward Bach, *Masonic lecture* (1936)

△ **This dense community of buttercups is perfect and will yield a high quality essence.**

on the day of preparation

Choose a clear and sunny day, as the mother tincture will require three to four hours of clear, unclouded sun to "cook" properly. Shower or bathe upon rising, using un-perfumed soap, and wear light-coloured clothes, particularly if you are sun potentizing. Arrive as early as possible, as the flowers must be picked by 9.00 am at the latest. Sit near the flowers and ask respectfully for permission to pick and to be drawn to pick the best blooms for making an essence. Finally, ask help from the elements to make this wonderful essence.

◁ **This wild heather location, far from civilization, will hold strong earth energies.**

Making a flower essence by sun potentization

Sun potentizing is the most favoured preparation method for essence makers. In the Bach system this procedure is used to prepare the Twelve Healers, Seven Helpers and White Chestnut. The flowering plants used are Agrimony, Centaury, Cerato, Chicory, Clematis, Gentian, Gorse, Heather, Impatiens, Mimulus, Oak, Olive, Rock Rose, Rock Water, Scleranthus, Wild Oat, Vervain, Vine, Water Violet, and White Chestnut.

△ **1** Rinse your hands in pure clean water. Place the glass bowl, being careful not to touch the inside, next to the flowers being used where it will receive full sun for up to four hours. Fill the bowl with fresh spring water and pull away any grass or leaves that might shade it.

△ **2** Cover the palm of your hand with a broad leaf. Quickly pick flowers on to the leaf, collecting them from all over the location. Touch the flowers as little as possible. Place the flowers on the surface of the water until it is completely covered. Leave in full sun for up to four hours, or until the flowers fade.

△ **3** When the correct length of time has passed remove the flowers from the bowl by flicking them off the water using a piece of stalk from the plant. Make sure that you do not touch the water with your hands.

◁ **4** If there is a lot of pollen or vegetable matter in the water, strain through an unbleached coffee filter paper, being careful not to touch the essence water.

▷ **5** Measure the quantity of mother tincture made and add a similar amount of brandy. Pour into a storage bottle and label. Save a small amount of any remaining mother tincture to taste and return the rest to the earth, giving thanks to the flowers for their healing gift.

Making a flower essence using the boiling method

The boiling method is used for preparing the Bach New Nineteen from the following; Aspen, Beech, Cherry Plum, Chestnut Bud, Crab Apple, Elm, Holly, Honeysuckle, Hornbeam, Larch, Mustard, Pine, Red Chestnut, Star of Bethlehem, Sweet Chestnut, Walnut, White Chestnut, Wild Rose and Willow.

◁ **Honeysuckle flowers ready for boiling.**

1 Wash your hands in clean water. Pour a little water into the bottom of the pan and, using long-handled secateurs (pruning shears), cut some perfect flowering twigs from all the trees in the immediate vicinity. A hooked walking stick can be used to pull down twigs to cut.
2 Recut the twigs to fit the pan until it is three-quarters full. Keep a sturdy stick to take home if you are not boiling the essence on site. Cover the pan with a lid and return home as soon as possible to boil, or boil on site.
3 Fill the pan with fresh spring water until the twigs are completely covered. Put on the lid and bring to the boil.
4 Remove the lid and press the twigs down into the water if necessary, using a twig from the same tree. Simmer for 30 minutes to reduce the liquid.
5 Leave to cool, outside if boiling indoors. Once cold, filter and bottle the essence as for the sun potentizing method.

Dilution and care of essences and equipment

As you learn how to make flower essences you will begin to build up your own store of mothers from which you make the stock and dosage bottles. Mothers are the pure essence you make on site from the distillation of flowers, sun and water mixed with brandy. Stock bottles are made from a dilution of the mother mixed with brandy, and dosage bottles are made up of water and a few drops from the stock bottle.

As your flower essence collection grows it is important that you give some thought to the equipment you use and the place where you store the bottles.

sterilizing essence-making equipment

It is vital that all equipment used for making an essence is sterilized to ensure that residual energies from previous remedies are completely eliminated. Dr Bach was so concerned with this factor that he used glass bowls only once, breaking them after use. They are so difficult to locate today that it is not practical to do this. A simple baby-bottle sterilizer is cheap to obtain and suitable for nearly all possible needs, although the inside may have to be customized.

The pans used for the boiling method may be too large to go in the sterilizer, so fill them with bottled water and leave to boil for 20 minutes, or invert them over a sterilizing pan and steam for 20 minutes. Remove while still hot and allow to dry on plastic lattice trays. Wrap in clean cloths and store in a dry cupboard.

All your essence-making equipment must be kept for this purpose only and should not be used for cooking or other domestic purposes. You should also use bottled spring water, not tap water, in the sterilizers and pans. Leftover water from the spring could also be used. Minerals from the water may build up on the equipment, so purchase a natural glass cleaner and polish them up once in a while before sterilizing.

◁ **Bottles can be used again if they are carefully cleaned and sterilized properly.**

▽ **When you are making up stock bottles give yourself plenty of time and space so that you can give the task the attention it deserves.**

sterilizing dosage bottles

To sterilize dosage bottles, purchase a new enamel or glass saucepan. Stainless steel is also suitable, though expensive, but aluminium is best avoided. The pan should be labelled and kept for this purpose only. Pour a little bottled water into the bottom of the pan and put in the bottles and pipettes, put on the lid and simmer for 20 minutes.

There is no need to sterilize the rubber teats and plastic caps, as the water does not reach that far up. Wash them in some soapy water, cleaning inside the teats with a small brush then rinsing several times with boiled water. You can complete this process by putting the bottles in a warm oven to dry, this ensures that they stay shiny. Left to dry normally there is often a residue. However, polishing while still hot prevents this.

preparing stock bottles

Mother tinctures are prepared by preserving the newly made flower essence tincture in an equal quantity of brandy. This mix will keep indefinitely and, as the stock strength is highly dilute, will last a very long time. To prepare a stock bottle, fill a 30ml/1fl oz dropper bottle with brandy and add 2 drops of mother tincture. This is the traditional dilution. However, two drops of mother tincture added to a 10ml/⅓fl oz bottle, which is the usual size of stock bottles purchased over the counter, has also been proven to work effectively. Mix well by banging the base of the bottle on the palm of the hand and allow to "stand" for a few days before use.

Instead of the stock dilution, 2 drops of pure mother tincture may be used in the dosage bottle if preferred. This was suggested by Dr Bach in his original instructions in 1936, and is an option for the essence maker.

storing flower essence mother tinctures and stocks

Careful storage ensures the potency and safety of your collection. A good course of action is to split the mother tinctures into two sets and store one of them away from home, perhaps with a friend or relative. This is the only way to ensure the safety of the collection in case of accidents. Wrap each bottle in paper or bubble wrap to prevent the vibrations merging and pack in a small box. Store

◁ To ensure that the essence-making equipment is not used for other things, keep it in a separate cupboard.

▽ Label your bottles as you make or mix them, don't rely on your memory for identification.

in a dry place, away from direct heat. Store the mothers for current use in a dry cupboard away from direct heat, strong smells or chemicals, ensuring the bottles do not touch.

These guidelines also apply to stocks, so store them in the boxes they were purchased in, or any other clean storage container. It is best not to stand stocks loosely, as they tend to be easily knocked over and roll about, often straight out of the cupboard to smash on the floor.

a workspace

It is important to keep the equipment you use for making essences separate from other utensils or tools. You might also have enough space in your home to dedicate solely to your flower essence work preparation and storage, but this is not essential.

labelling flower essences

Always label essences in full for later reference, however small your collection. Use a permanent pen, as spillage from the bottle

could make the label run. On the label you should include the date it was made or mixed, plus the contents and the location, in the case of mother tinctures. On dosage bottles, ensure the name of the person being treated is clearly written, to avoid any confusion in the household if more than one course of treatment is being taken.

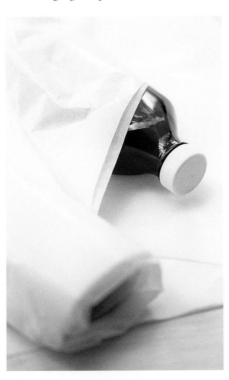

◁ Wrapping mother essences for storage keeps their vibrations clear and true, which guarantees the best results.

Other methods of essence preparation

There are many other approaches to making essences, not all of them using flowers. These preparations are better known as "vibrational" essences.

living flower or dipped essences

Some essence producers believe that picking the flowers is not necessary to making a flower essence, and use this approach. A spray of the living flowers is lowered into the bowl of water, the stalk being held down by forked twigs, threads tied onto sticks or crystals tied to threads. The tincture may be left to "cook" for quite short periods of time or for long ones, perhaps several days, usually decided by dowsing or intuition. The healing energy of the flowers is imprinted into the water just as effectively from the living flowers as from the picked ones. Some producers combine the two approaches and float picked flowers on the available water surface, in addition to having a living spray in the water.

variations on a theme

Many creative variations are used to make flower essences in this modern age. Some makers use a specific number of flowers, for example three, or seven. This is said to give results just as satisfactory as covering the whole surface of the water with flowers. A sunny day may or may not be chosen, as essences are now made in all different types of weather. Some producers make them during a clear night, allowing the essence to benefit from the moon or starlight.

Many producers use mediums other than water on which to float the flowers, such as oil or vodka. Normal instructions for making an essence are followed, but the essence will not need to have a preservative added, as it is already in a stable solution.

Water may still be the choice for the mother tincture, but other preservatives may be employed, such as glycerine or vinegar, which is helpful if the essence is destined for those who cannot tolerate alcohol.

Flowers may be laid in a pattern, or a

◁ When making a living essence, first see if the flower stems will stay in the bowl without assistance.

▽ Many environmental essences are made in Alaska and have a transpersonal quality that can enhance our connection to the planetary consciousness.

number of different varieties may be mixed together in the bowl to create some unusual, if one-off, potencies.

Alternative light sources such as lasers have also been used with success, and powerful essences have been produced by replacing the bowl with a geode, which is a hollow crystal structure.

△ Immerse natural crystals in a bowl of spring water and leave in sunlight. Dowse to see when the essence is finished.

▷ A recent and popular choice from the Pacific is an unusual range of essences made from sea creatures and shells.

environmental essences

Using many varied approaches, vibrational essences can be made out of anything natural, since all of nature radiates a life-force which can be harnessed for healing purposes. Essences made from crystals are the best known alternative, and a popular choice. Combination essences can also be made, mixing flowers and crystals, for example.

Some wonderful environmental essences have emerged, expressing energies such as stars, storms, snow, glaciers and even the aurora borealis. These are made by leaving a bowl of water outside during a storm or under the stars to absorb the vibrations. Alternatively, some snow or ice from the glacier is added to the bowl and left in the sun. The Bach essence Rock Water is also an environmental essence and is made in a similar fashion.

channelled essences

Following the beliefs of Native American "animal medicine", a range of animal essences are now available. These essences are produced by ritual and meditation in which there is an attunement to the animal spirits in the wild. The resulting healing energy generated is focused into the water, which is then preserved. Other forms of channelling are widely used. Some practitioners, often healers, will hold a bottle and project the healing energy into it, praying that it be made especially for the person in need. Provided the process is conducted with a very pure intent the results, although obviously subjective, seem to produce some good and certainly unusual essences.

▷ Gently hold the dosage bottles in your hands and channel energy into the bottle.

Prescribing Flower Essences

"To me the meanest flower that blows can give thoughts that do often lie too deep for tears."

Wordsworth

Conducting a flower essence consultation

Through the simple act of listening attentively to another person talk about their concerns, it is possible to select a mix of helpful essences. However, for consistent results some points are worth remembering.

the interview

Prior to the meeting, sit quietly, forget about personal commitments and ensure that you feel calm and centred. Consider doing a protection exercise and spraying some essences around the room.

Welcome the client with a drink and chat gently, to put them at their ease. If they do not know much about flower essence therapy, open the session with a simple explanation. Ask what it is they require help with and notice their tone of voice, as they speak. Match your personal body language to the client's in an unobtrusive way, and quietly follow them should they move. This technique, called mirroring, is designed to make the client feel more at ease. It is also an opportunity to experience how it feels to sit like them – are they tense, self-protective, aggressive or relaxed? Empathize with the client's story and imagine how they are feeling, allowing your intuition free rein. What is it communicating? Develop a caring, understanding atmosphere and mention the strengthening, supportive characteristics of the essences at different times during the interview. Many clients may not be ready to change. Dr Bach said there must be a change in outlook for healing to happen, so be careful not to make unrealistic claims. Encourage them to seek out other help if necessary.

Essences are chosen for how people feel about their difficulties and no attention is paid to their physical complaints in this system of healing. The resultant uplifting of the client's mental state may indirectly improve health, but the client should be encouraged to seek further expert help if appropriate. Note the predominant state of mind. Listen for keywords and pay attention if the client

◁ **Prior to the consultation, sit quietly, forget personal commitments and ensure that you feel calm and centered.**

▽ **Keep the area for making up essences clean and attractive.**

refers to them more than once. It may be easy to pick them out, or more information may be required. If so, ask questions about how they react to their life experience in varying situations. "How are you when you are tired? In a crisis? At parties? At work? When you are ill? In new situations?" Ask about past traumatic events. "Is there anything you have found difficult to cope with

The mind being the most delicate and sensitive part of the body,

shows the onset and the course of disease much more definitely than

the body, so that the outlook of mind is chosen as the guide as to

which remedy or remedies are necessary.

Edward Bach, *The Twelve Healers and Other Remedies* (1933)

▷ If the final choice
of essences seems
unclear, allow more
time to reflect.
Post the bottle to
your client the
following day.

◁ Some therapists
like to say a quiet
prayer of healing
intent over the
newly prepared
dosage bottle.

very detailed dosage instructions, not forgetting to remind the client that everything that has been said is confidential.

closing the consultation

Before the client leaves, they may consider booking a further consultation, since once the bottle is finished the contents may need to be reformulated. At that time, assess the client as if they were a new patient, as the Bach system works by viewing what is going on for them in the present. If progress is still being made, some of the previous essences may still be applicable. Other essences may be discarded and new ones added.

Clients like to be reassured that they can phone if they have more questions. Consider giving them specific times to call as this will set essential boundaries.

in the past? Do you like your job? Are you happy with the relationships you have with other people at home and at work? Is there anything else you would rather be doing in life? Are there any changes you feel are necessary to make?"

choosing the essences

To clarify if a certain essence is correct ask further questions using its complete symptom picture as a guide. "You seem to be the type of person that puts a brave face on things. Do you say you are fine when you are not? Are you the heart and soul of the party? Perhaps you enjoy a drink or two? Do you find it hard to talk about your feelings? Do you ever wake up in the night and feel restless?" These are the kinds of questions you might ask if you sensed you were talking to an Agrimony type.

During the interview explore what kind of personality the client has, hopefully picking out their type essence. This will serve to

support their individuality, which Dr Bach considered essential, and help them find greater overall strength and balance. It is not necesary for the client to present the full symptom picture in order for them to require an essence. Two or three strong indications are sufficient to suggest it as a possible choice.

Pick out the essences that would be helpful and share this with the client, checking whether they agree. Make the final choice together, this will help the client feel more responsible for, and involved in, their treatment. Throughout this process make sure that you focus on the positive aspects of the essence, if they appear too negative, the client may feel they are being judged. Encourage the client to use affirmations and stress the importance of developing a positive and forward-looking frame of mind, at all times. Label the bottle and give

▷ Ensure that all essences and necessary
equipment is on hand before the client arrives.

Using dowsing to choose remedies

Dowsing is a popular skill developed from the ancient technique known as water divining and is a useful way of choosing remedies. It is a method of connecting to the higher mind of an individual, which knows all things, by means of a pendulum.

pendulums

You can choose a pendulum made of wood or crystal, or use anything that is symmetrical and can be suspended from a thread or thin chain. A curtain pull may prove an inexpensive option. The pendulum is suspended over a set of essences or a list, and a yes or no question is posed. The pendulum will swing in a predetermined way to answer the question.

learning to dowse

In the beginning, it will be necessary to establish a yes or no dialogue with the pendulum, whose answer could be symbolized by a back-and-forth swing, or an anticlockwise or clockwise swing. Stillness can also be seen as an answer, but is more difficult to ascertain initially. There are many approaches to learning to dowse, but the following are reported to be effective.

method 1

Hold the pendulum's thread with your thumb and forefinger and make sure it is

△ **Pendulums made of wood, brass, stone or crystal are widely available. Experiment to find out which feels right for you.**

△ **Dowse over bottles, pictures or lists, and find out what works the best for you.**

still. Ask out loud, "What is the swing for no?" Keep repeating "No, no, no" in your head to encourage the pendulum. It may know immediately how it wishes to express itself, so observe carefully which way it begins to swing. Take time for this to become a strong and clear signal. Then still the pendulum and begin again, asking, "What is the swing for yes?" Take time to observe this while repeating "Yes, yes, yes" in your head. Should the results be vague, repeat this exercise several times over a period of days in the hope the results become clearer. However, if this process fails to work it is obvious that the pendulum needs to be taught to talk, so move on to method 2. The majority of individuals can learn to use a pendulum, so do not lose heart, but remain confident that a strong communication link will be set up, one way or another.

method 2

Decide what you want the swing for yes to be and "make" it swing that way, either mentally directing the pendulum, or by a slight action of the wrist. Then say, out loud, "This is the swing for yes." Repeat this exercise with the chosen swing for no. Once you are confident that the pendulum seems to know what it is doing, test whether this second strategy has been successful by remaining detached and, this time, without directing the pendulum in any way, say "Show me the swing for yes". If that is now clear, test the no swing.

If you are finding difficulty in starting, despite these exercises, you could try asking an experienced dowser to literally "hold your hand" when you first start – this often seems to work.

Once the pendulum has a strong and clear yes or no swing, it is important to test the link. A succession of foolproof yes and no questions, to which you already know the answers, will build your confidence, give you the opportunity to observe how responsive the pendulum is, and get the pendulum accustomed to swinging over from one reply to the other. Perhaps the pendulum would prefer to be stilled between each question. The only way to find out is to try, since each pendulum behaves differently. Some possible questions could be: "Is my name Mary? Is my name John? Am I a woman? Am I a man? Is my birthday in September? Is my birthday in March?" And so on.

dowsing for flower essences

When you are dowsing essences for someone it can be performed directly over the bottles of flower essences. While suspending the pendulum over each individual bottle ask, "Does (name) need this essence?"

Sometimes time can be saved by dowsing over a box of ten remedies, and asking "Does (name) need anything from here?" If there is a yes answer open the box and indicate three with the fingers and ask, "Does (name) need any of these essences?" If yes, then test for each one individually? It's quite safe to experiment, as it is possible to check progress at any stage by asking, "Is it right for me to dowse for (name)?", or "Are these remedies correct for (name) at this time?", or "Does (name) need any further remedies?"

A good question to ask throughout is "Am I influencing the pendulum?" as it is very important to check periodically during a dowsing session.

Asking the right questions is critical to successful responses and well-chosen essences. The more precise the question the better the answer. For example: "Which

▽ **When selecting successive bottles for regular clients, some dowsers get better results if they use a new witness each time.**

DOWSING FROM LISTS

Dowsing is a very flexible art and many individuals dowse from lists. This is a useful way of finding which essences may be required without buying them first. Simply dowse down a list, in the same way as over bottles, double-checking the results at the end. Read in detail about the chosen essences to confirm that they are a helpful choice. However, if the descriptions fail to resonate, the pendulum might be tuning into deeper levels of the being.

flower essences are most appropriate for (name's) personal growth and highest good at this time?", or "Which flower essences will be most helpful in improving (name's) stress/depression/fear/grief at this time?"

Once proficient in the use of a pendulum, the size of the swing can be cultivated to provide deeper information, for example a gentle swing for a little yes/no or a huge one for a big yes/no.

dowsing for others

Dowsing can be done on behalf of another person, whether they are present or not. Should they be present, it may be sufficient

△ **Pets are good subjects for dowsing and it may give valuable insight into their difficulties.**

just to have them sit nearby while the essences are chosen. Alternatively, suggest they touch the essence or box while it is dowsed: this will create a circuit of energy, which may improve results.

If the individual is not present it seems just as effective to link to the person, prior to dowsing, via a lock of hair or a picture. Some people prefer to use a blood spot. The pendulum is hung over the object, referred to as a "witness" while you ask if it is right to choose a selection of flower essences for that person. Providing the answer is in the affirmative, you can proceed as normal.

checking dosage instructions

Using dowsing, it is possible to check how many essences are needed for the dosage bottle, how many drops of each stock may be required, how many drops are to be taken, how often, exactly when and for how long. The resulting information may prove very different from the producer's instructions and the approach to be used remains a personal choice.

A note of caution: dowsing can prove so helpful and effective that it is easy to become lazy in learning about the essences in detail. This point has been discussed by producers and they conclude that the more knowledgeable the practitioner, the more effective the results, even with intuitive techniques such as dowsing. A fusion of counselling with intuitive techniques may prove to be an effective compromise.

Intuitive diagnosis

We all get gut feelings – about people, situations and places – and these feelings are nearly always correct, some would say they always are. Can you remember a time when you had a strong gut feeling and listened to it? Such as not going to work by the usual route, and later hearing about a traffic jam, or an accident? Most people can recall such instances, or perhaps have had the experience of knowing who is about to call before the phone rings. However, we have all grown up in a society where logic and rational scientific explanations rule the roost, and intuitive feelings are often disdained.

right and left brain

The brain has two sides, the right and the left. For nearly everyone, the left deals with logic and reason, attributes needed to deal with the physical world. Meanwhile, the right works with the intuitive skills of creativity, knowing (clear seeing), feelings and the ability to channel unconditional love. To activate the right side, the left needs either to be diverted, or quietened – which a daydream state does very nicely. Yet we were all told at school to "Stop daydreaming!" To a great extent, we have all grown up in a left-brain society, where neither feelings nor intuitive skills are valued.

Intuitive diagnosis is the developed skill of using the intuition to help find answers to particular problems. August Kekulé, the 19th-century chemist who spent many years searching for the formula of the structure of benzene, found one day that the answer just popped into his head while he was dozing in front of the fire. Later, to a gathering of important scientists, he said, "Let us dream, gentlemen, and then we shall find the answers to our questions."

Intuitive diagnosis is the art of tapping into inner knowing and inner feelings about a situation. Out of all possible solutions to a question, only one can be correct, especially if the question is put so the answer can be only "Yes" or "No". This explains how a pendulum works: it is acting merely as an external indicator of inner feelings – rather like the needle on a speedometer.

muscle testing or kinesiology

The technique of muscle testing, or kinesiology, can also help to obtain answers intuitively.

One simple method of muscle testing is to make a circle by joining the tips of the forefinger and thumb of your non-dominant hand (the left if you are right-handed, and vice versa). Then insert the forefinger and middle finger of the dominant hand into the circle made by the other hand. Ask a question, then try to break the circle of your thumb and forefinger, pushing them apart by separating the forefinger and middle finger. For a "Yes" or positive answer, the circuit usually breaks, as your muscles relax with a "good" feeling, while for a "No" or negative, the circle will hold firm, as the muscles stiffen slightly with a negative feeling. This is well worth practising with questions you know the answer to, like "Is my name …?"

questions

Having a clear question is, of course, crucial. So, as with pendulum dowsing, have a clear intention that the work you are about to do is for the highest good of all, especially that of the person you wish to help. Also be clear about whether in choosing flower essences to help this person, you wish to concentrate on present issues only, or on past issues as well, or perhaps also to look for essences to help deal with issues looming ahead.

Now still yourself, away from the clutter and the busyness of life, and allow yourself

◁ Although the method is simple, practice makes perfect. Look for the responses to questions you know the answers to.

ALTERNATIVE HOLD
An alternative method of muscle testing is to make a circle by joining the tips of the little finger and thumb of one hand, then holding the thumb and forefinger of the other together and inserting them into the circle made by the other hand. Try pulling your hands apart saying yes and no as you do so. Use whichever testing hold feels the most comfortable to you.

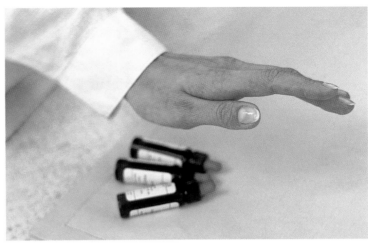

△ Some people already have the ability to feel different energies from different essence bottles, but it is a skill that anyone can learn.

◁ It is important to clear your mind of any clutter, and relax into a daydream-like state.

to relax into a daydream-like state. Next, ask the four starting questions, as for pendulum dowsing:

"Please show me a 'Yes'."

"Please show me a 'No'."

"Am I fit to dowse?" (you may be stressed, tired or otherwise out of balance).

"May we talk about ...?" This last question is vital, as it is inappropriate to use any intuitive skills without the permission of the person being asked about.

You may then ask "Are there any essences to create a balanced combination to help (name)?"

"May we choose the appropriate essence(s)?"

Then, using either a box of essences in front of you or, if you have the skill, a list of the essences, identify which essences to put into the treatment bottle, by asking about each in turn.

finding an essence

Intuitive diagnosis also includes two other methods. First, sometimes just by reading the description of an essence, you know it is right. Second, it is possible to choose essences by looking at photographs or pictures of a flower, or by cutting a pack of cards. It is most important, whenever you are choosing intuitively, always to read the essence descriptions and check that they apply. There may be occasions on which your intuition might be incorrect, and there is great value in learning about

yourself from the descriptions that come up.

Frequently, intuitive diagnosis can uncover important issues hidden – and forgotten – under the surface. A personal example may help. Andrew had used essences on a daily basis for several years when the essence Larch was indicated intuitively. Larch is for confidence. On the surface, Andrew, a competent doctor and family man, had no obvious need for Larch. However, after two weeks of taking it, he suddenly realized that his attitude to swimming had completely changed. Previously,

he had avoided it and made excuses. Now he had become an enthusiastic swimmer. What had happened? Andrew had learnt to swim in a cold pool aged nine at a time when he lacked confidence about life, having just started boarding school. Without his realizing it, that emotional climate had coloured his whole attitude to life – or at least swimming – until it was dissolved by two weeks of treatment: 30 years of hang-up gone in a fortnight!

Use your intuition, trust it, and learn from the answers it brings you.

◁ When choosing essences it helps to have a quiet space where you can easily feel relaxed.

A blossoming of essences

Many hold the view, which has some truth, that the Bach essences are all that is required to provide the support a normal household may require. However, in this age of global communications, life has lost much of its simplicity, but amazing new opportunities for technological advancement, personal and spiritual growth, knowledge and creative expression compensate for this. Unfortunately, these bonuses of modern life are set against a darker background of racial prejudice, unemployment, pollution, war, financial difficulties or family breakdown. Life can prove exceedingly stressful and can move so fast it almost seems possible to live lifetimes within lifetimes. These challenges push many individuals to their limits, and in response to this desperate need a vast blossoming of flower essences has arisen from every country of the globe, providing an enormous and overwhelming choice of healing opportunities.

◁ **This very tall, straight and exotic bloom, communicates a powerful doctrine of signatures.**

△ **A healing flower essence can be made from any plant in bloom.**

essences from indigenous flowers

Some people believe that it is better to take essences that are made from locally grown flowers, as the individual's personal energy will be more in tune with them. If that suggestion seems to ring true, then there will certainly be a selection of local companies providing a superb range of healing essences from which to choose.

choosing essences from around the world

Why not try a beautiful flower from Australia, the Amazon, the Pacific, the Himalayas or somewhere else equally exotic? There is a wide choice of interesting flower essences available from these faraway locations, but at first it might seem overwhelming to find the best choice from such a wide selection. Solve the dilemma this way: if there is a country that you have always wanted to visit or that has a special meaning in some way, you may feel closer to the

△ **Orange essence brings deep emotional release.**

△ **This red bloom has a dramatic message!**

the client, friend or family member to pick out the ones they are most drawn to and also the ones they most dislike, putting them in order. Then, discuss which of the strongest choices will be included in the treatment bottle. Alternatively, limit them to two or three of each. The results can be astonishingly accurate in expressing what the client most requires in an essence, and this is an ideal approach if the client is someone who finds it difficult to talk about their feelings. Used as part of the traditional consultation, this technique can add confirmation of the final choice and is a further way of involving the client.

▽ Lay out essences from a variety of countries and hold out your palm. Look up the descriptions of those that feel especially energetic.

spirit of the place by trying a flower essence made there. Alternatively, dowsing or using other intuitive techniques may suggest an appropriate choice of essences.

synchronicity
If all else fails, consider allowing synchronicity to provide the answer. That is, wait for a set of essences to turn up via friends, workshops, healing fairs, books, magazines or by surfing the huge volume of information on the internet.

Whatever ultimate choice is made, most individuals will respond positively to a well-chosen essence no matter where it comes from, or who made it. All essence makers are of the same breed – gentle spirits who are in love with nature, trying to help others in their own special way; much like the essences themselves.

choosing flower essences from pictures
An increasingly popular diagnostic technique is viewing pictures of the flowers, and many of the available books on various sets of flower essences have attractive illustrations that can be used in this way. Card sets of the Bach essences are easily obtainable, and are easier and more effective to use, since it is possible to see all the flowers at once. It is fun to lay them out and instruct

Treating yourself with flower essences

It is not easy to choose treatment for yourself, because humans are complex and it is often difficult to see yourself as you really are. However, it is helpful if you are to see the issues that require treatment and to understand how you need to be different. It may be easy to see surface symptoms, but harder to gain awareness of the underlying causes.

choosing an issue for self-treatment

Some lovers of essences never attempt to choose flowers for themselves, preferring to seek the advice of a fellow essence practitioner, and to do the same for them in return. However, making a commitment to treating yourself can provide a unique opportunity for personal growth, self-love and realization.

- Put aside the time to just "be" with yourself, perhaps through meditation or prayer.
- Take the time to step back and pay more attention to the ups and downs of daily life. If things could be changed to make life better, what would they be?
- Pose yourself the same questions you would ask a client as a useful exercise in self-treatment.

- Choose a single issue to work on rather than several. Select something that, if changed, would prove supportive to your life and in which improvements would be easily discernible.

time to change

Be ready for change, as often people say they are when they are not. True change may invoke pain and it could be that you unconsciously avoid it. Remember that essences give support and bring comfort during difficult moments. Read widely, aim to gain as much understanding about the flowers as possible, and see if any seem to be a match

△ **Taking time for self-care is not selfish. Nourishing our wellbeing ensures we can give love to others.**

◁ **Flower essences cannot effect a total transformation. Changes to lifestyle, for example diet, may also be required.**

▷ **Helpfully, flower essences can strengthen the desire to embrace a more healthy approach to life.**

for any specific issue. At first, you may think that all are needed since they represent the "human condition" and appear so familiar. Flower essences form a "language" by which you can understand others and yourself better. Perhaps the subtleties and nuances of feelings have never before been so clearly discerned, and can provide the fine shading which is essential to real self-knowledge.

the twilight zone

Many people have lost touch with their feelings and repress them into the unconscious, which is ultimately destructive to wellbeing. However, in the morning, just before you get up and click into the "daily face" – in that moment between waking and sleeping sometimes known as the twilight zone – your true-feeling state can be revealed. Pay attention to this and note down what those feelings are as this is invaluable insight into the most effective and healing choice of flower essence.

dreams as an insight to self-treatment

These same feelings can be expressed during sleep, in dreams. It is helpful to write these down upon waking, before the memory slips away. A consistent theme may repeat itself, which could suggest helpful essences to address some deep issues in need of healing.

ways to choose essences

With all this information in mind, finally make a selection of possible essences. If it appears there are too many, use some of the suggested intuitive processes, such as dowsing, pictures, or feeling the essences' energy, to narrow the selection down. Experiment with these different approaches and see if you get consistent results. At this point, talk to a friend and ask how they see you. Do the chosen remedies match their comments?

a flower essence diary

Be prepared to take successive bottles of essences, reviewing the combination after the end of each treatment. A diary can, over a period of time, provide useful insights into how the therapy is affecting you, insights which, if not noted down, may then be

◁ Reading past diary entries can be a helpful reminder of how far you have come, and which flower essences were particularly helpful along the way.

87

prescribing flower essences

forgotten. You are the best laboratory through which to experience and understand flower essences, which is essential if you are planning to help others.

using affirmation with flower essences for self-treatment

Be positive at all times: positive thinking attracts positive experiences and strengthens the immune system.

Many producers suggest repeating a positive affirmation each time a flower essence is ingested, enhancing the healing energy taken into the system and supporting change. This is a valuable self-help mechanism, as flower essences can assist in the positive reprogramming of negativity in the mind and emotions. Conscious co-operation improves the effectiveness of this process, since you are reminded, four times a day, to reprogramme the mind. Select affirmations that relate to the essences in the bottle or choose something general such as, "May all changes be for my highest good," or "I love and approve of myself."

The most receptive time to implant positive affirmations is 30 minutes before sleeping, since that is when the brain is at its most suggestive and also when the last daily dose of flower essences is taken, so never forget this opportunity. Writing affirmations out by hand is particularly helpful because in this way the critical mind can be bypassed and the positive suggestions go straight into the subconscious mind where, bit by bit, reprogramming can progress. Dreaming goes on to integrate these new patterns and clear out the old. Ten minutes of written suggestions of the right kind, before sleep, will provide positive and consistent reinforcement where it is needed.

The subconscious mind cannot distinguish between fact and fiction. It is simply programmed to perform in a certain way, keeping the individual confined within the limits of that paradigm. This is why it may feel so scary to change – since most of this programming was done during childhood, you are operating from some simple and outdated software.

Treating children with flower essences

Flower essences are ideal for children, as they are gentle and safe, but help positively with the difficult experiences encountered throughout the ups and downs of babyhood, childhood and adolescence. Remember that whenever you are using flower essences you are not in any way replacing conventional medicine, and that a doctor should be consulted for any symptoms of illness, especially in young children.

using essences with children

Children respond very quickly to flower essence therapy, as they tend to express what they feel more openly than adults. However, detailed discussion of problems may be

⊲ Patricia Kaminski of Flower Essence Services, California, says children respond well to the idea of calling essences Flower Drops or Flower Fairy Drops.

difficult, depending on the age of the child, so it is close observation on the part of the parent that provides the information for choosing suitable essences. Watching them while they play may be helpful, as this is when they will be showing their true natures.

Give treatment when they seem to be "not quite themselves", and talk to them about how they feel. Perhaps an active child has returned home from school sleepy and with no appetite, when normally she is

grabbing a sandwich and dashing out to play with friends. The correctly chosen essence, maybe Clematis in this case, can return her to her usual self, but you might also want to consult a physician.

Dowsing may assist in clarifying the best choice, but it is nice to remember that children may enjoy learning about flower essences and want to help choose their own. Picture cards are also an ideal approach with children, as they respond readily to the

⊲ Certain children can be so responsive to flower essences that two doses a day in a glass of water is sufficient.

▽ Putting some drops in a drink that they are taking to school as part of their lunchbox takes care of the midday dose.

POSSIBLE INDICATIONS FOR CHILDREN

indication	treatment
For help through puberty	Walnut
For being a victim	Centaury
For those who are bullies	Vine, Sunflower
For those who are over-active	Vervain, Bluebell
For those who are shy and timid	Mimulus, Borage
For help if they cannot learn	Chestnut Bud, Tansy
For those who lack confidence	Larch, Buttercup
For those who may be sulky	Willow, Self-heal
For those who are jealous of a younger sibling	Holly
For those who need constant attention	Chicory

striking colour images. Presenting the essences as something to help them settle in at school, sleep better or play football better will communicate the benefits on a level they can understand. Children will often remind you when it is time to take the flower drops again. Sometimes, older children can prove less enthusiastic, so adding essences to juice or milk can ensure they are receiving at least some of their doses.

treating babies

Newborns will benefit from 2 drops of Star of Bethlehem for the shock of the birth, especially if it was a particularly traumatic event with medical intervention. You could also add 2 drops of Walnut to help them adjust to their new life outside the womb. Drop these essences onto the crown of their head, or into their first bath. Should further treatment be needed, drops can again be put in the bath, or on to a breastfeeding mother's nipples. The mother can also take them herself, so the baby benefits through her milk.

◁ **Mild bumps, bruises, cuts and stings are a part of growing up. Flower essences in creams and compresses are soothing and quick acting.**

▽ **Make flower drops a part of bedtime. Tell stories about helpful flowers, and give some to a toy.**

If the baby is bottle-fed, a dosage bottle can be made up without brandy, and 4 drops added to the bottle. Flower essence drops can also be added to massage oil.

help for parents

Parenthood can be very stressful, particularly if it is for the first time. Tiredness from the birth and broken nights, the sudden responsibility, the onset of post-natal depression, all these difficulties can take their toll. Flower essences are a godsend at this time and can help to make parenthood more enjoyable. If there is a difficulty with a child, it is helpful to treat the parents as well, as the child could be reacting to their stresses.

USEFUL INDICATIONS FOR PARENTS

indication	treatment
To help the over-anxious parent	Red Chestnut
Wanting to be the ideal parent but cannot cope	Elm
Stressed-out and wanting to take it out on the child	Cherry Plum, Vervain
For complete exhaustion	Olive, Oak
Not able to face another difficult day	Hornbeam
Running out of patience	Impatiens
For the over-critical parent	Beech
For the possessive parent	Chicory

POSSIBLE INDICATIONS FOR BABIES

indication	treatment
For nappy rash	Emergency Essence Cream
For those that demand constant attention	Chicory
Helpful if they are very sleepy	Clematis
Comforting if baby is teething	Impatiens, Walnut, Chamomile
For those who seem over-sensitive	Mimulus, Yarrow, St John's Wort
Helpful when they have colic	Agrimony, Crab Apple, Chamomile
Useful if they are wakeful	Vervain, Bluebell and Chamomile
For those who seem susceptible to infection	Crab Apple, Pansy, Jack-by-the-hedge, Ramsons

△ **Crab Apple**

Treating animals with flower essences

Animals have feelings just like humans and can therefore suffer from a wide range of emotional problems. However, they do not always understand what is happening to them and cannot easily express to us how they feel except by what is thought of as antisocial behaviour. A certain amount of natural "wild" behaviour is normal, but notice what seems out of balance for the particular animal. The traditional approach to treating an animal is a combination of observation and empathy. Imagine yourself in their position, decide how they might feel about their life and choose essences to match that. Do not hesitate to consult a vet if your pet seems unwell or aggressive.

Animals are good subjects and respond very quickly to flower essence treatment, having fewer defences and a greater willingness to change than humans. This approach can rapidly bring their system back into equilibrium and they can become happier and more themselves.

animals are sensitive

Animals are affected by environmental pollution, the wrong diet, noise, city life, an unnatural living environment and a loss of connection with nature, just as humans are. If you have a strong bond with an animal, your personal stress levels could adversely affect it, as it is thought that animals can absorb negativity from their owners. If this seems to be the case, treat yourself as well as the animal, including some of the following:

EXAMPLES OF THE TRADITIONAL APPROACH TO TREATING ANIMALS

- A dog with its tail between its legs and cowering body language, who is nervous with new people and whines a lot, suggests a timid and fearful animal, so Mimulus would seem a good choice.
- A cat or dog who is around your heels all the time, who seems fussy and continually demands affection may need Chicory for attention-seeking behaviour.
- A dog who seems bad-tempered, and barks at everyone may require Beech for intolerance.

- Pink Yarrow: useful for animals that absorb the emotions of those around them. This essence protects and strengthens the aura.
- White Yarrow: for protection from environmental pollution such as car fumes and noise. This essence creates a shield of light which gives protection.
- Bluebell: for animals whose behaviour suggests that they are very stressed and are suffering from low spirits, with loss of a sense of self. This essence can bring peace, tranquillity, a reconnection with nature and the higher self.
- Chamomile: for tightness and stress in the involuntary nervous system, particularly around the digestive area. This essence can bring relaxation and calm.

△ **Animals may dislike brandy because it is aromatic. Use vodka, or no preservative.**

using essences for various animals

Flower essences are very easy to administer: put 4 drops in the drinking water, adding fresh drops when the water is changed. Additionally, put 4 drops on their food. For large animals, such as horses, put 12 drops in food and water. Alternatively, put the drops on a sugar lump or in a splash of milk.

If the animal is not eating or drinking at all, put drops on the fur so they can lick them off. If the animal is unconscious or too ill to lick, rub the essence around the mouth. If the animal is unapproachable, put 20 drops in a spray bottle with 50ml/2fl oz water and spray around them at least twice daily. This method was used successfully to treat a sick budgerigar who would not drink any water that contained essences.

A good tip is to spray small animals when it is time to clean out their home so they stay calm, and give the cage or hutch itself a spray before moving them back in. Walnut and Emergency Essence would be a good mix for this. Putting 2 drops into a fish tank will minimize the shock of changing the water.

FURTHER INDICATIONS FOR ANIMALS

indication	treatment
For animals who need help to learn new behaviours	Chestnut Bud
For adjusting to new circumstances, new home, family member or owner	Walnut
For the after-effects of shock resulting from fights, fireworks, accidents, thunderstorms	Emergency Essence.

Note: Flower essences are not a substitute for veterinary care.

Helping plants with flower essences

Flower essences are of benefit to all living things, including plants. As they require regular watering it is very little trouble to add some drops to the can and also to a spray when misting their leaves. They will become more resistant to pests or drought, and produce profuse growth and flowers. Vegetables may grow more vigorously and perhaps prove more tasty and nourishing.

The approach to treating plants is similar to that for animals or children: imagine how, as conscious beings, they might be feeling about what is happening in their lives.

Should they wilt a little try Wild Rose, and add Olive to give the roots strength to establish themselves quickly.

▽ **After repotting, water with Emergency Essence and Walnut to help the plant settle in.**

Cut flowers can benefit from a similar combination: Emergency Essence for the shock of being cut and Walnut so they settle into a new way of living. Again, give Wild Rose if they start to wilt, or Elm if it all appears to have been too much for the plant.

Oak may improve their resistance to infection and help them to stay well, in spite of a few pests being around.

Broken stems or branches have been mended using Emergency Essence cream smeared around the break, which is then bound up with tape or a bandage. Water the plant well with essences such as Sweet Chestnut, as it must have been an experience of great pain and anguish to be broken in half. Perhaps other essences would be helpful, so try tuning into the plant and see what ideas come to mind.

△ **Problems with pests and diseases respond well to Crab Apple in a spray.**

DOSAGE INSTRUCTIONS

- For a single treatment, 2 drops of each essence in half a cup of water, or 4 drops in a larger quantity.
- For long-term use, make up a dosage bottle and add 12 drops of the mixture per 4 litre/1 gallon can.

△ **Add essences to the can when watering seeds and young plants.**

FURTHER INDICATIONS FOR PLANTS

indications	treatment
If conditions are not right, the plant has given up and feels sorry for itself	Willow, Gorse
If the plant needs to stand up to pests or other plants taking it over	Centaury, Sunflower
If the plant seems diseased	Crab Apple, Ramsons, Jack-by-the-hedge
If there has been a setback in growth and the plant needs encouragement	Gentian
If the plant needs energy and strength to get started	Hornbeam, Elm, Olive

Flower essences on the journey of life

Flower essences can help you to feel more yourself, which is a natural feeling, like coming home, or remembering who you are after a period of forgetfulness. Some describe it as a sensation of relief, others as a kind of opening to the self, and all report feeling much better in themselves. Occasionally there may be a gentle release of emotion, and some tears may flow. Welcome them as a normal part of the healing process. Flower essences are not a quick fix and the effects happen gradually, as you are ready for them. This gentle, subjective process may sometimes go unnoticed, and close companions will often see the positive progress before you do. However, observations over a period of time make it possible to compare how you managed a situation before with how well you have dealt with a similar event more recently: you may be pleasantly surprised.

the path to individuality

Dr Bach believed that only when someone follows their true path in life would they find health and happiness. But having strayed too far, it can be impossible to know what is the best way forward. Take some Wild Oat, as this is known to bring insights into what may be the right path or, alternatively, into what is standing in the way, which may be fear, indecision or lack of confidence. Such problems can then be treated with the relevant flower essences.

△ **A natural meadow full of wild flowers, soaking in the power of the sun.**

QUALITIES OF FLOWER ESSENCE THERAPY

The following on-going benefits have been reported by many users:

- Feeling uplifted, calm, relaxed, happier, joyful; a state of relief and well-being.
- Improved resistance, health and vigour, youthfulness of mind and body, deeper feelings and emotional expression.
- Greater awareness of which activities bring increased joy and fulfilment.
- Assistance with the next steps in life, breaking through limitations and actualizing undeveloped potential.
- Achieving things that might once have proved difficult with greater ease.
- Listening to and trusting intuition, so that it becomes easier to find your rightful place in life.
- Staying centred and at your best, even in the midst of stressful situations.
- More conscious choice in behaviour, acting with awareness rather than reacting.
- Understanding more fully which issues, within and without, might need to be changed.
- Greater love and acceptance of the self.
- More sensitivity to nature and the simple pleasures of life, increased spiritual growth and awareness.

△ **Flower essences are treasured companions on the journey of life. When things are difficult, remember how helpful 2 drops can be.**

Perhaps your true calling was to be a carpenter, but life's circumstances have left you as an office clerk. Enrolling on a woodwork course can be a good beginning. Even as a hobby, if it is right, the activity will bring a sense of fulfilment and pleasure that will permeate the whole of your life circumstances.

Flower essences for strength and assertiveness

The greatest barrier to reaching your true path is often the people closest to you. They want you to stay the same for their benefit, so that they do not have to change. Consequently, there is a need to be doubly strong, first for yourself and second to stand up to them. The Centaury flower essence can bring strength to face such challenges with clarity and assertiveness. The addition of Mimulus and Borage for courage might prove helpful.

new beginnings

Never feel discouraged about the past, Dr Bach wrote encouragingly, or view it as lost time. Nothing that has been learnt is ever wasted and everything can be brought to good use in these new beginnings. In some way, everything is perfect, as even those who stand in the way of your progress become teachers and the situation ultimately proves a positive learning experience, teaching you more about yourself and how to be strong.

staying healthy

In the pursuit of good health and happiness, it is important to live a self-enhancing lifestyle. Unfortunately, society does not seem to support this, and it can often be an uphill struggle to achieve. Junk food, lack of exercise, overwork, no time for relaxation, smoking, drinking, staying up late every night, abusive situations such as domestic violence, co-dependent relationships or exploitation at work, prove common traps, particularly if self-esteem is low. Flower essences, in bringing greater self-realization, can help you to see that such behaviour is ultimately destructive and thus impress on you the desire to change. However, essences cannot, beyond the short term, support health so that life can continue in the same old way.

△ **Flower essences are wholesome and nourishing to the soul, as natural and healthy food is to the body.**

◁ **Help is always at hand. The familiar sight of little brown bottles scattered around the house can prove a real comfort.**

True health is not just the absence of disease, it is a "radiant" state. Life becomes more loving and joyful and living is fun. This happiness is infectious as everyone who comes into contact with you cannot fail to respond to such positivity and will leave your presence feeling uplifted and refreshed. Therefore, seeking true health is not selfish, it can be seen as a gift to a better, more loving and peaceful world.

treasured companions

The difficulties of life will continually challenge you to grow and become more today than you were yesterday. Flower essences are treasured companions on this journey of life and offer invaluable support and comfort. No matter how great or small the difficulty, flower essences will always be there to help. So relax and enjoy life, be happy, there is no longer anything to fear. Embrace the vision of Dr Bach.

Real health is happiness, and a happiness so easy of attainment because it is happiness in small things; doing the things that we really love to do, being with the people that we truly like. There is no strain, no effort, no striving for the unattainable, health is there for us to accept any time we like.

Edward Bach, *Free Thyself* (1932)

Recommended reading

recommended reading

Bach, Edward. *Heal Thyself: An Explanation of the Real Cause and Cure of Disease.* Saffron Walden, Essex: The C.W. Daniel Company Limited, 1988. First published: 1931.

— *The Twelve Healers and Other Remedies.* Saffron Walden, Essex: The C.W. Daniel Company Limited, 1988. First published: 1933.

Ball, Stefan. *The Bach Remedies Workbook.* Saffron Walden, Essex: The C.W. Daniel Company Limited, 1998.

Barnard, Julian and Martine. *The Healing Herbs of Edward Bach: A Practical Guide to Making the Remedies.* Hereford, England: Bach Educational Programme, 1988.

Barnard, Julian (ed). *Collected Writings of Edward Bach.* Bath: Ashgrove, 1999. First published: Hereford, England: Flower Remedy Programme, 1987.

Chancellor, Philip M. *Illustrated Handbook of the Bach Flower Remedies.* Saffron Walden, Essex: The C.W. Daniel Company Limited, 1991.

Cunningham, Donna. *Flower Remedies Handbook: Emotional Healing & Growth with Bach & Other Flower Essences.* New York, NY: Sterling Publishing Co., Inc, 1992.

Damian, Peter. *An Astrological Study of the Bach Flower Remedies.* Saffron Walden, Essex: Neville Spearman Publishers, 1986.

Devi, Lila. *The Essential Flower Essence Handbook.* Nevada City, CA: Master's Flower Essences, 1996.

Graham, Helen and Vlamis, Gregory. *Bach Flower Remedies For Animals.* Findhorn, Scotland: Findhorn Press, 1999.

Kaminski, Patricia. *Flowers That Heal.* Dublin: Gill and Macmillan, 1998.

Kaminski, Patricia and Katz, Richard. *Flower Essence Repertory: A Comprehensive Guide to North American and English Flower Essences for Emotional and Spiritual Well-Being.* Nevada City, CA: Flower Essence Society, 1986, 1987, 1992, 1994, 1996.

Kramer, Dietmar. *New Bach Flower Therapies: Healing the Emotional Causes of Illness.* Rochester, VT: Healing Arts Press, 1995.

Kramer, Dietmar and Wild, Helmut. *New Bach Flower Body Maps: Treatment by Topical Application.* Rochester, VT: Healing Arts Press, 1996.

Mansfield, Peter. *Flower Remedies.* London: Vermilion, 1997.

McIntyre, Anne. *The Complete Floral Healer: The Healing Power of Flowers through Herbalism, Aromatherapy, Homeopathy and Flower Essences.* London: Gaia Books Limited, 1996.

Petrak, Joyce. *How to Remember Bach Flower Remedies.* Warren, MI: Curry-Peterson Press, 1992.

Rudd, Carol. *Flower Essences: An Illustrated Guide.* Shaftesbury, Dorset: Element Books Limited, 1998.

Scheffer, Mechthild. *Bach Flower Therapy: Theory and Practice.* Wellingborough: England: Thorsons Publishing, 1986.

— *Keys to the Soul: A Workbook for Self-Diagnosis Using the Bach Flowers.* Saffron Walden, Essex: The C.W. Daniel Company Limited, 1988.

Shapiro, Jeffrey Garson. *The Flower Remedy Book: A Comprehensive Guide to Over 700 Flower Essences.* Berkeley, CA: North Atlantic Books, 1999.

Shimara. *Flowers of Life: Flower and Gem Essences for Healing and Spiritual Transformation.* Hoxne, Suffolk: Golden Ray Publishing, 1998.

Titchiner, Rose [et al.]. *New Vibrational Flower Essences of Britain and Ireland.* Halesworth, Suffolk: Waterlily Books, 1997.

Vlamis, Gregory. *Bach Flower Remedies to the Rescue: The Healing Vision of Dr Edward Bach.* Rochester, VT: Healing Arts Press, 1986, 1988, 1990, 1994.

Weeks, Nora. *The Medical Discoveries of Edward Bach, Physician: What the Flowers Do for the Human Body.* Saffron Walden, Essex: The C.W. Daniel Company Limited, 1983. First published: 1940.

Weeks, Nora and Bullen, Victor. *The Bach Flower Remedies: Illustrations and Preparations.* Saffron Walden, Essex: The C.W. Daniel Company Limited, 1964, 1990.

White, Ian. *Australian Bush Flower Essences.* Findhorn, Scotland: Findhorn Press, 1993.

Wildwood, Christine. *Flower Remedies: Natural Healing with Flower Essences.* Shaftesbury, Dorset: Element Books Limited, 1992.

Useful addresses

The Flower essences that are referred to in the book are available from the following producers.

Bailey Flower Essences
Arthur Bailey
7/8 Nelson Road
Ilkley, West Yorkshire LS29 8HN
Tel: 01943 432012
Fax: 01943 432011
email: baileyfe@aol.com

British Flower and Vibrational Essences Association
8 Willow Glen
Branton, Doncaster DN3 3JD
email:bfvea@greenmantrees.demon.co.uk

Light Heart Flower Essences
Rose Titchener
The Duke,
Chediston Green
Halesworth, Suffolk IP19 OBB
Tel: 01986 785242
email: Rose@Titchiners.freeserve.co.uk

Harebell Essences
Ellie Webb

P.O. Box 7536
Dumfries DG2 7DQ
Southwest Scotland
Tel/Fax: 01387 261962

Healing Herbs Ltd
Julian Barnard
P.O. Box 65, Hereford HR2 0UW
Tel: 01873 890218
Fax: 01873 890314
email: healing-herbs@healing-herbs.co.uk
www.healing-herbs@healing-herbs.co.uk

Ilminster Essences
Dr Andrew Tesidder
Yarn Bar, Sea
Ilminster, Somerset TA19 0SB
Tel: 01460 57475
email: andrew@flowers.force9.co.uk
www.Dr-Andrew-Flowers.co.uk

Sun Essences
English Flower Essence Company
Vivien Williamson
P.O. Box 728, Norwich NR6 6EX
Tel: 07000 785337
email: sunessence@aol.com
www.sun-essences.co.uk

USA
Flower Essence Services
Richard Katz and Patricia Kaminski
P.O. Box 1769
Nevada City

CA 95959, USA
Tel: 530 265 0258
Fax: 530 265 6467
email: fes@floweressence.com
www.floweressence.com

Master's Flower Essences
14618 Tyler Foote Road
Nevada City
CA 95959
Tel: (916) 478 7655
Fax: (916) 478 7652

AUSTRALIA
Nature's Energy
105 Glebe Point Road
Glebe NSW 2037
Tel: (02) 9267 8509
Fax: (02) 9267 4719
email: inquiry@adyar.com.au
www.adyar.com.au

Australian Bush Flower Essences
45 Booralie Road
Terrey Hills,
NSW 2094
Tel:(61) 9450 1388
Fax: (61) 9450 2866

Index

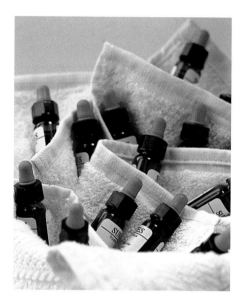